21ST CENTURY MANAGEMENT

Also by Mats Lindgren

BEYOND MOBILE (*with Jörgen Jedbratt and Erika Svensson*)

THE MeWe GENERATION (*with Thomas Fürth and Bernhard Lüthi*)

SCENARIO PLANNING (*with Hans Bandhold*)

21ST CENTURY MANAGEMENT

Leadership and Innovation in the Thought Economy

Mats Lindgren
CEO, Kairos Future

palgrave
macmillan

First published 2012 by
PALGRAVE MACMILLAN

Palgrave Macmillan in the UK is an imprint of Macmillan Publishers Limited, registered in England, company number 785998, of Houndmills, Basingstoke, Hampshire RG21 6XS.

Palgrave Macmillan in the US is a division of St Martin's Press LLC, 175 Fifth Avenue, New York, NY 10010.

Palgrave Macmillan is the global academic imprint of the above companies and has companies and representatives throughout the world.

Palgrave® and Macmillan® are registered trademarks in the United States, the United Kingdom, Europe and other countries.

ISBN 978–0–230–29789–0

This book is printed on paper suitable for recycling and made from fully managed and sustained forest sources. Logging, pulping and manufacturing processes are expected to conform to the environmental regulations of the country of origin.

A catalogue record for this book is available from the British Library.

A catalog record for this book is available from the Library of Congress.

10 9 8 7 6 5 4 3 2 1
21 20 19 18 17 16 15 14 13 12

Printed and bound in Great Britain by
CPI Antony Rowe, Chippenham and Eastbourne

To Jacob and Andreas

The future is like a stray dog. Whoever catches it gets it.

CONTENTS

List of Tables and Figures   x

Preface   xiv

About the Author   xvii

Introduction   xviii

1	**FRAGMENTS OF CHANGE**	**1**
	THE MASTER OF FOLLOWING THE ACTIONS	2
	FOLLOW THE ACTIONS, AND YOU'LL GET TO THE TRUTH	4
	SWALLOWING SWORDS IS THE ROAD TO FAME?	5
	WATCH OUT FOR PIVOT	6
	MAKING SHEEP FLOAT	7
	IN SEARCH OF EDEN	8
	IT'S A BIG NUMBERS WORLD	10
	IN THE LAND OF RESPONSE	11
	MEDICAL SCIENCE MADE REAL	12
	STOP VIOLENCE	13
	CONNECTING FOR A BETTER WORLD	15
	THE INTERNET DOESN'T LIE	16
	BUSTED!	17
	THE END OF CONTROL	19
	GO WITH THE CONSUMERS	20
	THE NEXT GAME-CHANGING DEAL	21
	BEING INNOCENT	22
	DON'T BORROW, JUST STEAL	24
	A GIANT LEAP FOR MANKIND	25
	THE ART OF SCORING	26
	HAND AND MIND IN PERFECT HARMONY	28
	NO MORE HUMAN DOMINATION?	29
	THE CALL FOR THINKING	30
	BACK TO BASICS	31
	LIFE IN THE ANTHILL	33

CONTENTS

THE RETURN OF THE MEGA-PROJECT 34
THE NEW ORIENT EXPRESS 35
ROOM FOR THE NEW METROPOLITANS 37
BUILD YOUR DREAMS 38
THE RACE TOWARDS THE FUTURE 39
HOW CHEAP IS CHEAP? 40
THE BOTTOM IS THE NEW TOP 42
NO MORE TRICKLE DOWN 43
THE END OF LOCAL 45
THE POWER OF POLITICS 46

2 **A NEW PARADIGM EMERGING** **48**
A COMPLEX WORLD 52
BUILDING THE JAMMING ORGANIZATION 55
CHOOSING PERSPECTIVES 59

3 **THE THOUGHT ECONOMY** **60**
THOUGHT-CELLS AND THOUGHT-NETS 61
THE CRY FOR THOUGHT LEADERSHIP 65
FIVE PRINCIPLES FOR SUCCESSFUL MANAGEMENT 66
ARE YOU FIT FOR THE FUTURE? 68

4 **JAZZING UP THE DATA** **73**
THE VALUE OF DATA 74
MEASURING PERFORMANCE DRIVERS 75
INSIGHT EXCELLENCE 78
DANCING WITH THE DATA 87

5 **WALTZING INTO THE FUTURE** **90**
GETTING TO THE FUTURE FIRST 91
CHANGE EXCELLENCE 92
DANCING WITH THE FUTURE 102

6 **GETTING INTO THE SWING OF THINGS** **105**
PLAYFUL THINKING, SERIOUS PLAYING AND GENEROUS
GARDENING 106
INNOVATION EXCELLENCE 107
DANCING WITH IDEAS 114

7 **IT TAKES TWO TO TANGO** **116**
WHAT'S A GOOD JOB? 117
THE IMPORTANCE OF KEEPING YOUR TEAM HAPPY 120
ENGAGEMENT: THE ORGANIZATIONAL GOLDEN EGG 121
TALENT EXCELLENCE 126
DANCING WITH THE TEAM 137

CONTENTS

8 DANCING CHEEK-TO-CHEEK   **139**
    SALES EXCELLENCE   141
    DANCING WITH CUSTOMERS   149

9 BUILDING THE JAMMING ORGANIZATION   **151**
    THINKING, LINKING AND BLINKING IN THE T-ECONOMY   151
    21ST CENTURY LEADERSHIP: BUILDING FUTURE CAPITAL   152
    FUTURE CAPABILITY CAPITAL   156
    FUTURE MARKET CAPITAL   158
    FROM STRATEGY TO ACTION: THE FUTURE CAPITAL MODEL   162
    BUILDING A JAMMING ORGANIZATION   166

Notes   168

Bibliography   187

Index   195

LIST OF TABLES AND FIGURES

TABLES

2.1 The paradigm shift from the Old World
to the New World   49

2.2 The four levels of external complexity   55

4.1 Aspects of operational efficiency   77

5.1 Strategic choice behavior according to
Fiegenbaum et al.   101

7.1 The traits of a good job according to
people in different countries   118

FIGURES

I.1 The required focus shift   xxii

2.1 External complexity induces internal
complexity   53

2.2 The jamming organization behind
strategic flexibility and performance   58

3.1 The evolution of societies, from raw
material era to thought era   62

3.2 The three-level Thought-net and its
Thought-cell (in black)   63

3.3 The five future-capabilities or T-habits   68

4.1	The cornerstones of insight excellence	79
4.2	Example of output from an analysis of Chinese blog posts about luxury	81
4.3	The 50 patent clusters with the highest annual registration of patents in mainland China	83
4.4	The relation between overall performance and an open mind	86
5.1	The path towards shaping the future	92
5.2	The cornerstones of change excellence	93
5.3	The relation between overall performance and systematic opportunity scanning	97
5.4	The relative importance of different time horizons now and then	99
6.1	The cornerstones of innovation excellence	108
6.2	The relation between overall performance and rapid implementation	109
6.3	The innovation machine	111
6.4	Organizational practices driving performance	113
7.1	Share of employees thinking that they're currently in their dream job, by industry	117
7.2	Work satisfaction as a function of influence, commitment and affirmation	121
7.3	Attitudes and preferences of young people over the decades	124
7.4	The Engagement tree	125
7.5	The cornerstones of talent excellence	127

7.6 Propensity of recommending one's workplace as a function of trust in supervisor 129

7.7 What people try to find out about a workplace before applying for a job 131

7.8 The buts of becoming a manager 133

7.9 Cultural differences in work-life-balance preferences 134

7.10 The relation between overall performance and clarity 136

8.1 The evolution of economic value 141

8.2 The cornerstones of sales excellence 142

8.3 The relation between overall performance and process focus 143

8.4 Modern markets demand a lot of its participants 144

8.5 The relation between overall performance and collaboration 146

8.6 A plan of action guided by the strength and complexity of your offer 148

9.1 The four aspects of a Future Capital process 154

9.2 The internal capabilities that build Future Capital 158

9.3 The Trend and Innovation Management Process (TRIM) 159

9.4 Future Map by the Nordic division of Kraft Foods in the early 2000s 161

9.5   Examples of outcomes from the Kraft
       Foods TRIM-process   161
9.6   Setting up a Future Capital Navigator   165

PREFACE

The idea of writing this book has evolved over many years. When I left my position as a research engineer at the Royal Institute of Technology in Stockholm in the mid-1990s after a short but intense period as an environmental researcher and teacher, I dedicated my life to the future. I didn't realize that back then, but in retrospect it's obvious.

In the mid-1980s I founded my own company, and starting writing, speaking and consulting on trends and how to manage companies and organizations in turbulent business environments. I developed a methodology to make groups more creative future thinkers, to separate probable from preferred and possible future and divergent and creative from convergent and analytical thinking, and to turn trends and scenarios into ideas and action. I studied the history of visions and envisioning, and the necessity of visions of values in organizations and synthesized my research and consulting experience in a method that later became known as TAIDA.[1] I also tried hard to keep up to date with the latest trends and wrote books on topics as various as the future of information technology, the future of work and the changing values systems among young generations.

Almost ten years after I left my position at the Royal Institute of Technology I realized that the time had come for something new. Kairos Future, a strategy consultancy based in strategic foresight was founded. Soon we were a small team doing more or less the same type of work I had been doing on my own. But we were also able to scale up, and the team grew to a company. We brought clients together around strategic future topics such as the future of the Internet, the mobile Internet, and tomorrow's marketing, leadership, schools, global values systems, universities and B2B sales. And we assisted clients in understanding the challenges ahead or in improving their *innovation machine*.

As time passed, I slowly developed an urge to test my hypotheses on performance drivers scientifically, and in the late 1990s I joined a doctoral program where my dissertation focused on strategy-related performance drivers in turbulent business environments. That was as close to 'the future' as my professor – Patrick Joynt at Henley Management College – allowed me to go, and I'm grateful for his solid advice. The dissertation sparked a new stream of research and research-based consulting within the company. We no longer based our advice and consulting services solely on secondary research and consulting experience. Piece by piece we developed substantial research on performance drivers in today's volatile business landscape, and finally put the results together in an integrated concept on leading and managing companies and organizations in today's business world.

Over the years I've come to the conclusion that many companies and organizations suffer from 'future-deficit'. In comparison to how much effort companies tend to spend on *managing the past*, very little is spent on *managing tomorrows*. We tend to face the future with closed eyes at best, and normally with the back of our heads first. While many larger companies have fairly smooth processes for dealing with ongoing business, very few have processes that are as tailored to identifying and managing future opportunities, despite the fact that these are the processes most significantly related to long-term performance. The consequences of this future-deficit is obvious, on both corporate and national levels.[2] Consequently, this book is a summary of several decades of thinking, research and consulting on the relationship between the organization and its environment or future environment. The ambition isn't to be all-embracing, but to provide a framework that the reader might use as a starting point on a journey forward.

The book in itself has been a long journey and I would like to take the opportunity to thank all my colleagues and clients who actively contributed to the ideas, models and concepts in this book through challenging questions, inspiring talks and endless discussions over the years. Especially, I would like to thank my editorial assistant Kira Repka, who helped to turn notes, outlines and unfinished chapters into a readable book, and my research colleague Björn Ljung, who has been a tremendous sidekick in many of the research projects presented in this book. Finally, thanks to my wife Christina, who has patiently withstood all my ideas and late hours over the years. Without her support, there would never have been neither a book, nor a journey.

Mats Lindgren
Shanghai, November 30, 2011

ABOUT THE AUTHOR

Mats Lindgren is the founder and CEO of Kairos Future Group – the leading future strategist in Northern Europe. He is a frequently hired international speaker on future-related topics and has over the years given more than 1000 speeches in more than 15 countries in Europe, North America and Asia. Lindgren holds master's degrees in engineering physics and human services and a doctoral degree in business administration, his specialty being strategic management in turbulent business environments. Mats Lindgren is also the author and co-author of more than 20 books on futures research and strategy methods, creativity, values, lifestyles and media, including *The MeWe Generation* (Bookhouse Publishing, 2005), *Scenario Planning* (Palgrave Macmillan, 2003, 2009) and *Beyond Mobile* (Palgrave Macmillan, 2002).

INTRODUCTION

> If the exponential growth of complexity
> were to continue, one week in 2025 would
> be as rich in milestone events as the entire
> 20th century.
>
> Theodore Modis, US business analyst,
> physicist, and consultant[1]

In the fall of 1986 I bought my first Apple computer. It was
the newly released Macintosh Plus – a wonder-machine with
1 MB RAM and 800 K floppy reader. In the US it was priced
at USD 2600, but in Sweden prices were higher, inspiring
entrepreneurs to start parallel import of Macs. With a con-
nection to the Royal Institute of Technology, my former
employer, I was allowed to buy the computer at the special
price of SEK 40,000 – more than twice its price in the US.
On top of that came a 20 MB hard drive with a discounted
price tag of SEK 20,000. In February 1988 I also completed
the set with a LaserWriter Plus, just as it was being replaced
by a new series of laser printers. This time the discount
price was the same as for the Mac, SEK 40,000.

A few years later, I attended an American master's program that was partly run in Sweden. I worked on the master's thesis together with a future colleague of mine who
lived 200 km north of Stockholm, and it was tricky to send
material back and forth. During the most intense part of
the thesis writing I was doing the stats on my Mac in my

home office using an ancient version of the statistics program SPSS, while my colleague was working from his home in Forsbacka 200 km north. SPSS wasn't very fast, although compared to the Digital VAX-computers I had used ten years earlier finishing my master's in engineering physics it went quite smoothly.

The problem was neither the statistics nor the clock speed. The problem was how the text most easily could be shipped back and forth between the southern suburbs of Stockholm and Forsbacka. The modem was the solution to our problems, and those of you who have ever used a classic modem to connect over the predecessor of Internet know what I'm talking about. This was something exclusively for teenage backyard hackers – not for consultants in their 30s or 40s – and required large amounts of both skill and patience. But remember when we start looking ahead that we're not talking about the Flintstone era. We're talking 1991.

NEW FOCUS

Have you ever had the feeling of being completely clueless? Are you wondering why young people know more about your business environment than you do, even though you've spent most of your life in it and they haven't? Then chances are that you're trying to tackle the New World in an old fashion. As we all know, the worlds of technology, economics and politics to name a few have been quite turbulent since 1991. Just like Theodore Modis concluded in the early 2000s when analyzing the increasing complexity since the Big Bang and the projected future of complexity: we're living in times of change. The result of the past 20 years of change is a whole new era of competition. As failure rates rise and business survival becomes harder due to increasing complexity,[2] managers and organizations are faced with new challenges. Unfortunately, what used to work doesn't anymore. And young people have an advantage since they've never known anything else than today's reality.

What we need is in fact a radical focus shift: from micro to macro and from internal to external focus. Introverted and shortsighted businesses were successful when the nature of the economy was introverted and shortsighted too. However, as new technologies have eliminated the struggles that I faced during my thesis work in 1991, the same technologies among many others have gradually transformed the world to a much smaller place than it was before. This New World places a whole new kind of pressure on managers. In an extroverted economy with longer and longer time horizons being considered, businesses have no choice but to follow. Thus the new era creates a cry for the externally oriented outward-looking organization, as illustrated in Figure I.1.

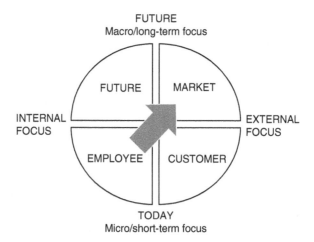

Figure I.1 The required focus shift

THE FUTURE STRATEGIST

Changing your organization's focus according to the new needs can however not be done overnight. Furthermore, trying to do so by the hand of the CEO may stifle business performance for a long time as his or her primary attention should go towards leadership and problem-solving in everyday production. Also, such a solution usually means that the required focus shift only takes place in PMs and presentation slides. My opinion is therefore that instead of taking the huge risk of a haphazard focus shift, a new specialist is needed: the future strategist. This new consultant or colleague is a person that can manage the company's strategic futures through moving swiftly between different disciplines. Understanding marketing as well as innovation and R&D, and strategy as well as HR, the future strategist knows what to do next – and in the step after that one.

MAKING PEOPLE DANCE

This is a book about the future. But it's also about the past and the present. Understanding your future begins in the past, so we'll start our journey by exploring the changing business landscape of the 21st century and what it means for organizations. Then, I'll present a new paradigm for how to think about and handle the complex world of business from a managerial and innovative perspective, so that you can increase the thought productivity in both yourself and in your organization. In the second part of the book, I'll give tips and tools for motivating and engaging your team, clients and customers in the quest for successful competition on the edge, so that you can get to the future before anyone else does.

Making People Dance isn't just the sub-title of this book but also is an affirmation or mantra that, if kept alive, will help you bring the best out of yourself and your organization. It serves as a constant reminder of the importance of building a *jamming organization* – and what that is will be explained in the following chapter.

1

FRAGMENTS OF CHANGE

> If you don't know where you're going, it
> doesn't matter which way you choose.

Times are changing, that's for sure. There are numerous
examples in business and society indicating that things
aren't what they used to be. Issues connected to globalization, shifting of powers, increasing turbulence and changing values are heading the news nearly every day. But
what's really going on, what does it mean to business and
society and how does the business community respond to
what's happening? And is there a general pattern, a pattern that can help us orient ourselves properly, develop the
skills needed and understand what it takes to get to the
future first? I think so, and in this chapter I'll start with
the fragments – the examples of what's coming and how
companies are adapting to what's next.

The drivers behind the New World, as described in
the 35 case studies below, are many and closely twinned.
Depending on what we're interested in describing, we can
choose several alternative perspectives. In short, however,
there are three large, long-term trends playing out in
the present that are at the core of the process we're now
witnessing: democratization of technology, education,
and homogenization driven by transparency. Naturally,

these aren't the only important components to keep in mind when facing the future. Topics such as energy and finance are only briefly covered in this book. However, the patterns of *how* and *why* things change are the same no matter how we turn this outward kaleidoscope. The overall picture that emerges through these images – as in other fields – is one of increasing complexity in terms of business context, customer relations and organizational structures.

After summarizing the central movements and tendencies from the real-world examples, I'll continue by putting this context into context, providing an outline of a new, emerging paradigm called the T-economy. T stands not only for the combination of spanning networks, focus and concentration (or Targeting) but also for the content and process – the Thoughts and Thinking – that are the prime drivers in this emerging economy. Thought (the process of thinking) and thoughts (ideas, mental pictures, reflection and intention) is what seem to be the key performance drivers and differentiators in the new business landscape. But let's start with the fragments and then continue with the general pattern.

THE MASTER OF FOLLOWING THE ACTIONS

Amazon owns the Internet
Front page of *Wired Magazine*, December 2011

The envy of all other e-commerce marketers, *amazon.com*, was founded in 1994 – the very, very beginning of Internet – by Jeff Bezos, who had a background in computer science and finance. (Netscape released the web-browser that was the beginning of surfing and browsing in 1994.)

Amazon launched its site in 1995, but contrary to most other so-called dotcoms from the end of the 20th century, Amazon chose a slow-growth strategy, building the company step by step and not intending to show black figures in the first four years. When the dotcom-bubble burst and many e-commerce companies went bankrupt, Amazon persevered. It showed its first black figures in the fourth quarter of 2001.

Amazon's rigorous approach is quite different from how most other players in the online retailer field act, and it's this foundation that makes them one of the top-converting websites month after month. Almost since the very beginning, Amazon has had an entirely data-driven strategy aimed to help both the customers (*People that bought this book often bought these too*) and the company itself (since those kinds of tips simply drive sales). Compared to most other online retailers they've made analytics and following the actions of their customers a core strategy, and have therefore built a culture of website optimization as their main asset. While studies indicate that over 75 percent of their competitors don't do any optimization testing at all,[1] Amazon doesn't belong to those that just pray for luck. Instead, they apply the same concept that made Toyota so successful, treating change as an evolutionary process where innovation is driven by small alterations. Even Amazon's *add-to-shopping-cart*-button is thoroughly tested and under constant scrutiny!

For Amazon, success comes from a continuous cycle of optimization, so what you need to do is to figure out how you can create your own cycle of measuring, refining and testing. Remaining curious is one of the drivers behind Amazon's success and, as the next section will show, a property that may help you stand out from the crowd.

FOLLOW THE ACTIONS, AND YOU'LL GET TO THE TRUTH

> To profit from good advice requires more wisdom than
> to give it.
>
> John Churton Collins, English literary
> critic (1848–1908)[2]

At *okcupid.com* – one of the leading dating sites in the
US – 7 million active users[3] can take tests and find the
perfect match just like on other dating sites. Founded by
Harvard students Chris Coyne, Christian Rudder, Sam
Yagan and Max Krohn, who gained recognition for their
creation of *thespark.com* (featuring a number of humorous
self-quizzes and semi academic personality tests, including
the four-variable Myers-Brigg style Match Test), OkCupid
has its origin in SparkMatch. Allowing registered users who
had taken the Myers-Brigg test to search for and contact
their type of peers, SparkMatch became popular and was
launched separately and later renamed OkCupid.

What really makes OkCupid different though isn't
its history but instead OkTrends: original research and
insights based on hundreds of millions of OkCupid user
interactions. Using the OkTrends data, OkCupid is able
to determine what works in the world of matching and
dating – and we're not talking interest lists or occupations
here, but more sophisticated analysis. For instance, how
should a photo be arranged in order to optimize the probability to get a conversation going from a message sent or,
frankly speaking, the probability that someone would be
interested? The data reveals that you should be *doing something interesting* in the picture, preferably *with an animal*,
and you should definitely not be *drinking* or having *fun with
friends*; nor – god forbid – should you use your 'MySpace

shot'. And if we know what works, we can become more successful by following those actions.

Compared to Amazon, OkCupid may be in the beginners' league. Still, they're ahead of the pack and – according to a recent MIT study[4] – they'll probably stay there. This international study of 3000 top executives shows that the best prepared in terms of applying analytics as a performance strategy are the ones most eager to use even more data and analytics in business. And knowing what to do with data is definitely a good skill when meeting the future.

SWALLOWING SWORDS IS THE ROAD TO FAME?

A sword is useless in the hands of a coward
Nichiren Daishonin (1222–82)

You may have seen him in TED conferences, on YouTube or in the newspaper – the Swedish professor and sword swallower Hans Rosling talking about our common future, accompanied by moving bubbles on the screen.[5] Rosling is definitely a performer, and one who follows the guidance of the above quote. But is it the swords that are the foundation of his fame, making him an international celebrity and sought-after speaker? Well, it probably helps, as gimmicks are always welcome in the art of stage performance. However, the formidable success of Hans Rosling and his creation Gapminder is in the moving graphics and holistic approach that enables him to narrow down a century of human history in just a few minutes.

It all had began when Rosling, Professor of International Health at Karolinska Institutet in Stockholm, wanted more efficient methods to get his message across. Boring PowerPoint presentations with bullets and diagrams wasn't enough when he wanted to paint the big picture of human development and public health to his students, his academic peers and business and political communities. Together with his son and his daughter-in-law, he started experimenting with software solutions to convert international statistics into interactive and enjoyable graphics, aiming to promote a fact-based worldview based on public statistics. Rosling's presentations were an immediate success, and in March 2007, Google acquired the Trendalyzer software to be used in their Motion Chart Google Gadget and Public Data Explorer. But as we're about to find out, Rosling (and now Google) isn't alone. He is just a pioneer of one of the greatest trends in the world of data, namely multi-format visualization and organization.

WATCH OUT FOR PIVOT

Seeing is believing

At another TED conference – the one in Long Beach, California in February 2010 – Gary Flake, head of Microsoft's Live Labs, enters the stage and asks '*How do you take a big collection of things and make sense out of it?*' In the following six minutes he provides a response in the format of a presentation that resembles no other. On the screen behind him, Flake sorts huge amounts of information, zooming in and out, selecting and filtering at remarkable speed. In just six minutes we learn about mortality, that Flake is a Lance Armstrong fan, about the most popular topics on Wikipedia, and a lot more. But most amazing of all: it's all in images. Visual and *real*.[6]

The software that Flake used for his presentation is called Pivot and was at the time unreleased. It used a dataset from Wikipedia but presented it in a much more attractive and efficient way than ever seen before – an instant success because no matter what era we live in or which tools we use, *attractive* and *efficient* will always be at the core of all presentational skills. So when the world of data changes, with increasing computing power allowing for larger and larger amounts of data to be considered, pedagogics simply has no choice but to follow suit.

What Gapminder and Pivot both show is the future of data processing: user friendly, intuitive, powerful and amazing. And that future is here now. We don't linger on texts and figures anymore but are instead able to play around with large amounts of data in ways that it wasn't even possible to imagine just a few years ago. And that will not just change how we play with data. It will change the way in which we look upon the world, and also what we expect from those presenting the world to us.

MAKING SHEEP FLOAT

Who said math is boring?

Have you ever wondered if Jesus is larger than Buddha in London, or where the US Methodists have their stronghold? Have you ever thought of how bars are related to the relative frequency of escort services, or in which US state you can buy the cheapest weed? You don't have to wonder anymore: just visit *floatingsheep.org*. Based on data from Internet searches, blog posts, yellow pages and other Internet present data, Floatingsheep – a playful semi-academic project by geographers Matthew Zook at the University of Kentucky and Mark Graham at the Oxford Internet Institute at University of Oxford – maps the world, based on 'a little theory and calculation'.

What Floatingsheep shows is that, based on what's already out there, we can retrieve huge amounts of intelligence using open and unstructured sources such as blogs, tweets, Facebook, comments in discussion groups and so on, and then summarize the results in graphics that are very easy to interpret. But while the team behind Floatingsheep probably just wanted to do something fun and meaningful, to others – first and foremost Google – a world of accessible data means business and severe cost cutting. Instead of sending out millions of questionnaires asking people about their religious beliefs, just take a look in Facebook and you'll know for sure. But don't try to go through it manually. Even though data is openly accessible to almost everyone there's too much of it to process without sophisticated tools. This means that, at least for now, the advantage belongs to those who know how to automate search and analytics. And that includes my own company.

IN SEARCH OF EDEN

> By listening to consumers in the blogosphere we may continue to develop innovative products that allow gardeners around the globe to create their dream gardens.
>
> Margareta Finnstedt Möller, former
> Global PR Manager of Husqvarna[7]

In 2009 Kairos Future set out on a journey together with the garden equipment producers Gardena and Husqvarna to find the lead consumers of their markets. The mission was to explore the drivers of modern gardening as expressed by passionate gardeners that we identified through social media where they express their view of the world everyday. We used computer software to analyze 1.4 million blog posts in 13 markets across the globe, then manually browsed through thousands of them, and finally checked Internet searches related to gardening to see whether what's at the heart of true garden-lovers holds for the general public too. And what we found was thrilling.

Husqvarna Global Garden Report 2010[8] presented the top gardening trends across the globe, derived from close study of the people who really know what gardening is about. Although most of them wouldn't personally describe their passions and efforts as an attempt to recreate Eden, this is exactly what they're doing if we aggregate their behavioral patterns. In traditional mythology, Eden represents the unspoiled place of perfect harmony, away from the dangers and noise of the world. But since Eden is our dreams' desire, the image of Eden varies from person to person, as therefore do the dreams of the perfect garden. The dreams of Eden are also influenced by the zeitgeist and culture, meaning that the *recreated Eden* varies across the globe and over time.

What's great about blog analysis is that it allows for spontaneous association, meaning that we can get answers to questions we wouldn't have known to ask in a survey. Even though we're working our way through massive amounts of qualitative data, aggregation is still feasible. The shift that makes it possible is basically driven by the combination of social media, the accessibility to large amounts of data and increasing computing power. In Chapter 2 we'll see that this computational power is one of the prerequisites for the emergence of the New World. However, it can also be used for purposes that are perhaps of lesser importance, but yet impressive.

IT'S A BIG NUMBERS WORLD

Feelings are the path to life

In August 2005, Internet artist and designer Jonathan Harris and computer scientist Sam Kamvar came up with a new idea in the spirit of Audre Lorde, who once said that our feelings are our most genuine path to knowledge: they are chaotic, sometimes painful, sometimes contradictory, but they come from deep within us.[9] People feel sad and people feel fine. But when and where, and who feels what? *'Do women feel fat more often than men? Does rainy weather affect how we feel? What are the most representative feelings of female New Yorkers in their 20s? … What were people feeling on Valentine's Day? Which are the happiest cities in the world? The saddest? And so on.'* Those were some of the questions that Harris and Kamvar asked, and out of a sudden the solution to their problems presented itself: the blogosphere.[10]

Every few minutes, their system searches cyberspace for newly posted blog entries including the phrases *I feel* and *I am feeling*, recording the feelings (happy, sad, addicted and so on) in such sentences. Since blogs largely have the same structure, personal information such as age, gender, geographical location and so forth can be identified and saved along with both the sentence and the local weather conditions from the point in time when the post was written. As a result, Harris and Kamvar now have a database of several million human feelings, increasing by 15,000–20,000 new feelings per day.

Harris and Kamvar's ambition was artistic rather than scientific or commercial, so they built a website – *wefeelfine. org* – that presents the results in an attractive and self-explanatory way. Every feeling posted is represented by a single dot or particle with a color and a size that represents the nature of the feeling. The particles careen wildly on the screen and if you click on a specific one the sentence or photo it contains is revealed, but the particles can also be asked to self-organize around any number of axes expressing human emotions. And classification of emotions can be used for more scientific purposes as well.

IN THE LAND OF RESPONSE

Let there be granted to the science of pleasure what is granted to the science of energy; to imagine an ideally perfect instrument, a psychophysical machine, continually registering the height of pleasure experienced by an individual.

Francis Ysidro Edgeworth, Irish economist
and philosopher (1845–1926)[11]

Have you ever heard of the Mappiness project? You might not be alone. When I write these lines, I've only been part of the Mappiness community for a couple of weeks. Every now and then I get a push to my iPhone where I'm asked to respond to a series of questions regarding my happiness, relaxedness and sleepiness. In return I get quite a lot of statistics about my own happiness, from which I've already learned that I'm most happy at work, in meetings, between 12 and 2 pm on Fridays. From the Mappiness website I've learned that I'm one of approximately 22,000 contributors, mostly from the UK – many of whom provide photographs from happy moments that are displayed as a map on *mappiness.org.uk*.

The Mappiness project was initiated in August 2010 by a team at the London School of Economics[12] with an ambition to better understand how features of peoples' current environment – features such as air pollution, noise, and green spaces – affect their feelings. To do so they developed an iPhone App through which the contributors several times a day deliver data on their present mood and activities. Since the iPhone is location sensitive the project is also able to collect location data automatically, which enables the researchers to link the happiness to location and – indirectly – to temperature, weather, light and pollution from other data sources. So in the New World, emotions and experiences are simple natural sciences and can therefore be quantified as such. Edgeworth's psychophysical machine is here.

MEDICAL SCIENCE MADE REAL

Medicine isn't what it used to be

In 1998, Stephen Heywood was diagnosed with amyotrophic lateral sclerosis (ALS). As their brother got worse, James and Benjamin Heywood saw that patients with specific and rare diseases are often left on their own: it's hard to find information, there are few people to share experiences with, and the patients themselves need to be the experts of their own symptoms since professional expertise is rare. In 2005, the two brothers therefore launched a site aimed at helping patients with ALS connect and share their experiences. Since the start, PatientsLikeMe has so far also included communities for multiple sclerosis (MS), Parkinson's disease, fibromyalgia, HIV, chronic fatigue syndrome and mood disorders, as well as the rare conditions progressive supranuclear palsy, multiple system atrophy, and Devic's disease (neuromyelitis optica). Users access *patientslikeme.com* for free, and in September 2011 the site had more than 115,000 members suffering from more than 500 different conditions.

It's the conversation and collection of data that makes PatientsLikeMe so unique and revolutionary. As people report on their medication and health-conditions, large amounts of real-world data is aggregated – data that's not possible to collect in other ways because researchers don't even know what to ask for. Since about 15 percent of the users choose to share information not only with fellow patients but also with non-members, physicians and researchers accessing the site can find out what treatments patients have tried and how successful they were. PatientsLikeMe has itself both introduced a series of research projects that analyze clinical information given by the patients, and initiated partnerships in clinical research with pharmaceutical companies such as Eli Lilly and Novartis.[13] So it is not surprising that Business 2.0 and CNN Money named PatientsLikeMe one of '*15 Companies that Will Change the World*'. And making a change is really what it's all about, isn't it?

STOP VIOLENCE

> Twenty years from now you will be more disappointed by the things you did not do than those you did do. So throw off the bowlines. Sail away from the safe harbor. Catch the trade winds in your sails. Explore. Dream. Discover. Give yourself away to the sea of life.
> Mark Twain, US author and humorist (1835–1910)[14]

In the late 19th century people didn't believe in telephones because only the king, the prime minister and a few rich people would ever have them. But the number of telephone subscribers kept rising and passed the turning point, and out of a sudden everybody needed one. The same happened with the telefax in the mid-1980s and with e-mail accounts ten years later. In the mid-2000s it was time for Facebook: another example of Metcalfe's law. Named after engineer Robert Metcalfe, one of the inventors of the Ethernet, it stipulates that the value of a network is proportional to the square of the number of participants in the network. The larger your network and the larger their networks are, the more probable it is that one of your contacts knows *somebody*. And that's the power that is making Facebook, LinkedIn and Google+ so popular.

On October 7, 2007, a few boys started arguing at a high school party in Stockholm, and what started as an argument ended with a boy being kicked to death in the street. Five teenagers were arrested, and four of them convicted of murder. One of the partygoers – Anton Abele, a 15-year-old first-year student – was upset with what happened and decided to take action. Wanting street violence to end he launched a Facebook group called *Stoppa gatuvåldet* (followed by an English group: *Stop Street Violence*). In less than 24 hours the group had 3000 members, and a week after the tragic event, manifestations in respect to the victim Riccardo Campogiani were held in Stockholm, Gothenburg and Malmö in Sweden, and Copenhagen in Denmark. Tens of thousands attended the events, and the interest was so big that the Stockholm manifestation had to be moved twice.

Abele's Facebook group soon had 112,000 members, and on November 1 – less than a month after Campogiani's death – Abele was granted the Free Your Mind Award at the MTV Gala in Munich, Germany. Since 2010 Abele has been the youngest ever member of the Swedish parliament. What he did was to use social media to connect, interact and build relations – connections that did and continue to do good. A few years later followed the Arab Spring, where social media played an important role in bringing down non-democratic governments.

CONNECTING FOR A BETTER WORLD

United we stand, divided we fall.
Classic motto attributed to Aesop (620–564 BC)

In 2003 Mohammad Yunus – Grameen Banks founder, father of microfinance and 2006 Nobel Peace Price laureate – visited Stanford Business School as a guest speaker. Jessica Jackley worked at the school and invited Matt Flannery, who had never before heard of microfinances, to the lecture. Shortly after, Jessica started a career as a consultant for the nonprofit Village Enterprise Fund, helping to start small businesses in East Africa. Matt visited her in Africa and they spent time interviewing entrepreneurs about the problems they were facing. After returning from Africa, the couple began developing a plan for a new type of microfinance concept built on the idea of connecting borrowers and lenders over large distances. In 2005 they started the non-profit organization Kiva, which means *unity* in Swahili.

At *kiva.org*, entrepreneurs in need present themselves and their businesses. Lenders can choose a borrower, after which it takes merely a few clicks to complete the loan. But although Kiva might appear to be a peer-to-peer organization, it's actually even cleverer than that. Borrowers and their needs are promoted on the Kiva website, but technically the loans have already been accepted by one of Kiva's 138 field partners when the requests for a loan are posted – local partners who are thus kept in the business of helping others. So in actual fact you don't lend to Maykell Neftaly Bravo Campos directly. Instead, the system ensures that he gets funding as soon as he needs it, because (as we all know) timing is crucial in business – no matter if it's a huge Western enterprise or a single motorcycle taxi in Nicaragua.

Over its first six years Kiva has transferred USD 240 million in loans to 625,000 borrowers in 216 countries, with a repayment rate of almost 99 percent. And since we're talking microloans, the average loan is less than USD 400, and even sums of as little as USD 25 are gratefully accepted.[15] But while Jackley and Flannery used the Internet as the foundation of a new form of social entrepreneurship, the Internet holds destructive powers too.

THE INTERNET DOESN'T LIE

No business opportunity is ever lost. If you fumble it, your competitor will find it.

Anonymous[16]

For a time, if you Googled United Airlines, one of the first hits you got was to a YouTube clip: *United breaks guitars*. If you haven't yet seen it, please do.[17] Then compare United's YouTube presence with that of Southwest Airlines, who have made a case for personality and individuality, thus creating a cascade of video clips of rapping flight attendants that are quite appealing.[18] The comparison shows the consequences and power of social networking and online rating, because the difference is essentially one man: Dave Carrol.

In March 2008, Dave Carrol was on tour with his band. When Dave looked out the window waiting for takeoff from O'Hare Airport, he saw ground personnel throwing luggage – including his custom-built guitar. After leaving the plane, Dave was in a hurry and didn't report the guitar being damaged. When he did so a week later, he was told that it was too late to do anything. For nine months the case was chewed over by the United Airlines machinery, and to the last person who said no Dave made a promise to write three songs that would be released worldwide. *United breaks guitars* was posted on YouTube on July 6, 2008, and within ten days it was seen by three million people. Customers cancelled their tickets while others chose alternative airlines, and United soon came crawling, offering Dave free flights. But Dave said no: he was now signed and had become famous. Instead, he published his next video.

United breaks guitars raises questions of authenticity and fact. Did United actually break the guitar? Who were the people who started the avalanche? And what has it cost United? Nevertheless, it's a vivid illustration of the world of social media and of its brutal impact on business. But it's also a reminder of how critical employees are in the branding process. If the complaints handler hadn't so rigorously followed the rules none of this would have happened to United. In fact, employees are no longer only a company's greatest assets: they're also its biggest risks.

BUSTED!

Playing with brands is a 21st-century amusement

One evening in April 2009, Kristy Lynn Hammonds, 31, and Michael Anthony Setzer, 32, working at Domino's Pizza in North Carolina wanted to have some fun. After work they started playing around with the food, sneezing in it, stuffing their noses with cheese and so on, recording everything they did and said. When they finished playing around and turned the camera off, they published the video on YouTube, creating the buzz of the week. Millions of people watched the video more or less instantly, and observant customers quickly notified Domino's Pizza. Just day after the video was released, Hammonds and Setzer were unemployed and Patrick Doyle, the CEO of Domino's, apologized for what had happened in a second video, also thanking the observant customers.[19] Unfortunately, that response has only received viewed a fraction of the views of the Hammonds and Setzer post.

Besides consumers taking control over brands and employees constantly risking them there are also – to make matters worse – more professional activists intently trying to change the brand image of companies. The most renowned is probably the Canadian Adbusters, a non-profit anti-consumerist organization founded in 1998 by Kalle Lasn and Bill Schmalz in Vancouver. They describe themselves as 'a global network of artists, activists, writers, pranksters, students, educators and entrepreneurs who want to advance the new social activist movement of the information age'. And they do. Besides publishing the reader-supported *Adbusters* magazine, which has 120,000 subscribers, Adbusters is known for its *subvertisements*, which spoof popular advertisements. A favorite object is McDonalds, having been granted several campaigns. Adbusters has also initiated several international activist campaigns, such as the Buy Nothing Day.[20]

So the question is: what do you do to shield yourself from blows such as the ones that United, Domino's, McDonalds and others have taken? Well, there's of course no way to make your company immune as long as you're not willing to get rid of both your employees and your customers (which I'm quite sure that you aren't). However, humility to the fact that you're no longer in charge of your own brand will help.

THE END OF CONTROL

> To dare is to lose one's footing momentarily. To not dare
> is to lose oneself.
>
> Søren Kierkegaard, Danish philosopher
> and author (1813–55)

'Search this: Fujitsu ScanSnap Scanner S300 Reviews.' This
text, accompanied with a picture of the scanner in question, filled a page in the November issue of Wired magazine
in 2008. Below, in a smaller font, the ad said: *Do a quick
Internet search to check out the reviews.* So what point was
Fujitsu trying to make with this ad? Were they so certain
about the reviews that they thought they could rely on
them? That they didn't even need to tell the good news
about their scanner themselves? Maybe, maybe not. The
effect was nevertheless that Fujitsu showed their customers
and potential customers that they

- Understand them
- Don't underestimate them
- Know that their customers will be searching anyway
- Understand that customers don't trust ads
- Understand that they're *owned* by their customers
- Show that they're willing to be their customers' loyal
  servants.

With that, Fujitsu's 2008 ad summarizes the essence of the
new consumer society logic: brand owners are no longer
in charge. Customers and users build the brand just as
much as it is built by PR agencies, advertising wizards and

marketing departments. It's what the consumers do with your products and what they say about them that in the end builds the brand. So what could be better than actually making them part of the product development process as well? In fact, doing so is exactly what turned LEGO from a company with severe financial problems to a company that's now performing at its best for a very long time.

GO WITH THE CONSUMERS

> The trouble is: If you don't risk anything, you risk even more.
>
> Erica Jong, US author and poet[21]

A few weeks after the launch of LEGO Mindstorms in 1998, Kekoa Proudfoot, a PhD student at Stanford University, broke the code of RCX and brought it all out on the web.[22] The community (70 percent of whose members are adults) started to write new programming languages for Mindstorms and one person even came up with a new operating system, LegOS. Programming became easier and a third-party supplier started to produce Mindstorms-compatible sensors that were far better than LEGO's originals. But for the LEGO headquarter in Billund (Denmark) this was tricky as they had a tradition of strongly protecting their property rights – not just for the money, but also for the matter of reputation, since poor copies risked destroying the brand. Luckily, they realized that the hackers made Mindstorms even more attractive, blessing LEGO with a self-sustaining community of users. Consequently, LEGO rewrote the program license and added a *right-to-hack* clause. And it was a hit. Version 2 of Mindstorms is LEGO's all-time bestseller.

Next, four US hackers were invited to a top-secret round-table discussion in Billund. The Mindstorms User Panel had to pay its own airline tickets, and all they got in return were some plastic bricks. The panel then spent ten months advising LEGO. It expanded to 14 members, and shaped what the new robots will be able to do and which parts come in the kit. The latest Mindstorms has little in common with its predecessors except for the name: it has fewer pieces, the computer itself (NXT) looks like an MP3-player rather than a piece of LEGO, and the program is free for downloading from LEGO's website. What the user panel brought in and what was developed by the LEGO-staff is hard to tell, but Mindstorms NXT was a great success and was number two on the American boys' Christmas list, right after Nintendo Wii. And that wouldn't have been possible if the management of LEGO hadn't been extraordinarily open and unconventional – as were Procter & Gamble.

THE NEXT GAME-CHANGING DEAL

> An idea that is not dangerous is unworthy of being called an idea at all
> > Oscar Wilde, Irish writer and poet (1854–1900)[23]

What do you do when your innovation rate is flat while costs climb faster than top-line growth? That was the challenge facing Procter & Gamble's R&D director Larry Huston in 2000.[24] Like most other R&D managers in mature, innovation-based companies, Huston faced increasing competition and an exponentially growing demand for more and better innovations. But unlike most others, Procter & Gamble started thinking, and thinking differently. Its newly appointed CEO, A. G. Lafley, realized that growth objectives couldn't be met by spending more and more on R&D for less and less payoff. Therefore, he challenged Huston to reinvent the company's innovation business model.

Historically, the best innovations had come from cross-fertilization or by connecting ideas across departments. But could that model be extended even beyond the company's borders? After a study of acquired products the answer was clear: external sourcing of ideas and products could produce highly profitable products as well. Huston estimated that on every internal researcher there were 200 scientists and engineers elsewhere that were just as good, so with their new approach the research organization could multiply from 7500 to 1.5 million. Based on that insight, Lafley set the goal that half of the products should come from their own research labs, and half *through* them.

The core of the new model is the *Connect+develop* website where individuals or companies can submit their proposals while Procter & Gamble can advertise their innovation needs. And their invitation to submitters is indeed tempting: *'Could your innovation be the next game-changing deal?'*[25] Within a few years of its launch, the company had increased innovation productivity by 60 percent and was more than halfway to the 50 percent goal. At the same time, the R&D spending as a percentage of sales had gone down from 4.8 to 3.4 percent. But if Procter & Gamble could find 1.5 million innovators, researchers and engineers just within their field, how many more could there be in total?

BEING INNOCENT

Nothing is impossible to a willing heart.
John Haywood, English Playwriter
and Poet (1497–1580)

What if you could connect all the innovation seekers of the world with all the innovation solvers out there, and create a global market place for innovations? Surely many have tried, but only a few have succeeded. Among those is Alpheus Bingham, founder of InnoCentive. Since the start in 2001, 250,000 solvers have registered at *innocentive.com* and – strikingly – half of 1300 challenges posted have also been solved so far.[26] The process is straightforward: seekers in need of solutions post open challenges with a fee connected to each problem, and solvers whose solutions are selected by the seekers are compensated for their ideas by InnoCentive, which acts as broker in the process.

In the late 1990s, theories about open innovation were brought forward, focusing on the need for organizations to involve all stakeholders – customers, end users (consumers), employees, external partners and problem solvers – in the innovation process. But when large companies begin to apply open innovations approaches, the large numbers challenge quickly surfaces. What if a company with 100,000 employees launches a platform where internal solvers can post ideas and anyone with a problem can advertise their needs? How would you manage such a huge market place? For solutions with a seeker it's pretty easy, but how about all the loose ideas that nobody has asked for? Even if every employee produced only one new idea per year, this still adds up to 100,000 ideas floating around. How would you sort them? By tags? By topic? By size? And how do we see in which areas there are plenty of ideas, and where there are few?

A pioneer in the field – Swedish telecom giant Ericsson – has an internal ideas management platform with tens of thousands of ideas and comments, engaging several thousand employees.[27] Employees are encouraged to post and vote for ideas, and solutions-seekers post their problems or innovation needs on the platform, asking solvers to come up with solutions. Welcome to the world of ideas, and not only the world of *big* ideas but of a big *number* of ideas! This is why we need the analytics and visualization mentioned earlier, because while you don't necessarily have to invent, you need to be conceptually innovative. In this world where information, ideas and even patents are abundant commodities there's still much to be done with these components. Seeing the picture and making it is what matters.

DON'T BORROW, JUST STEAL

Opportunity makes a thief.
Francis Bacon, English Philosopher (1561–1626)

In October 2001, Apple changed the world of music even though its executives a few years earlier had sworn never to get into consumer electronics again. As the company started developing software for digital devices, Steve Jobs realized that existing digital players were clumsy, useless and ugly. It then took Apple less than a year to develop a completely new product line, and the secret behind their speed was to use existing resources instead of inventing everything themselves.

To start with, Apple didn't invent the hard drive player. Creative – the Singaporean market leader – had launched one in 2000. The idea of a hard drive player linked to a system where users could legally download music came with Tony Fadell, a former General Magic and Phillips engineer who approached Apple after being turned down by Phillips. The MP3-format was bought from the Fraunhofer Society, while the software was based on PortalPlayer's not yet released reference platform. Not even the iTunes concept was Apple's idea. In 2000, before Fadell approached Apple, the company purchased SoundJam MP – the basis for iTunes. Apple just added an Applish user interface and deleted some functions that didn't fit their business model. Good artists borrow, great artists steal, Jobs used to say, referring to Pablo Picasso.[28] And that's exactly what Apple did.[29]

What the Apple team did was to bring the pieces together.[30] With big-picture thinking so characteristic for Steve Jobs and Apple, they were able to see what nobody else saw. And with a little help from other friends – the passionate Apple clan, willing to buy anything at any price as long as it's released by Apple – they were also able to generate the revenues needed to get the iPod going. The rest is history.

A GIANT LEAP FOR MANKIND

Without creativity a manager may do a good job, but he cannot do an outstanding one. At best he can preside over the progressive evolution of the organization he manages; he cannot lead a quantum jump – a radical leap forward. Such leaps are required if an organization is to 'pull away from the pack' and 'stay out in the front'. The creative manager makes his own breaks.

Russell L. Ackoff, US organizational theorist, consultant and professor (1919–2009)[31]

Once upon a time there was this idea that we were living in a big-leaps world. Then came the Toyota way (and the Scania way and all the other ways following the same principles). To the West, that was an entirely new way of running things. The USA in particular had a tradition of strongly focusing on revolutionary leaps in innovation rather than on kaizen and continuous improvement, and it wasn't really until the 1970s that US carmakers realized that they were betting on the wrong horse.

Innovation is essentially an evolutionary process, and that applies to everything from software development to biology (or from Bill Gates to Charles Darwin, if you will). But of course, leaps are necessary too. Constant improvements and kaizen are never going to revolutionize the world. They will make it better, yes, and in the long run also very different. But they will not provide us with the big shifts. However, another form of evolutionary process can: recombination, as we've seen in the iPod case. And recombination requires the application of a certain mindset and some radical thinking. Without breakthrough thinking, the world would never have seen the wheel or the computer, and that's irrespective of whether we consider them to be evolutionary or revolutionary innovations (because I guess that we could argue that all innovations have elements of both in them). And what we're in fact about to find out next is that breakthrough thinking begins in breakthrough action.

THE ART OF SCORING

> We are what we repeatedly do. Excellence then is not an act, but a habit.
> Aristotle, Greek philosopher, student and teacher (384–22 BC)[32]

Kalmar is small Swedish town on the Baltic Sea that for 300 years was the center of a union between Sweden, Norway and Denmark. But those days are long gone, and Kalmar is now a sleepy town with 30,000 inhabitants. Kalmar doesn't have much and can't even boast great athletes like its neighbors Nässjö (where multi-athlon star Carolina Klüft was raised) or Västervik (the home of tennis legend Stefan Edberg). But Kalmar has soccer (or football, as it's called everywhere except for the USA).

Kalmar FF, the local team, had been up and down in the national league but never really made it until coach Nanne Bergstrand was brought back in 2003. Bergstrand based his philosophy on kaizen, which in his world meant never to look at the number of goals but instead focus on the game and the performance in the field. Knowing that the team producing the most chances wins in the long run, Bergstrand was happy as long as the team followed the tactics and produced chances, and dissatisfied if the team won and scored several goals but played poorly and won by mere luck. Four rounds into the season of 2008 Kalmar reached the top position in the league and kept it until the end. For the first time in history they were the champions. This wasn't just a victory for Kalmar FF and the team, but also for the city of Kalmar, which honored Bergstrand by naming one of its streets after him.

What Bergstrand and his philosophy did was to help the team focus on what in management terms would be called the *process*, *practices* or *behaviors* rather than the end results, which in a performance-oriented industry such as sport is rare. Of course we need to celebrate victories – probably more than we often do. But we shouldn't, as Bergstrand shows us, be discouraged by failures. We should analyze and reflect on them to see whether anything could have been done differently, but we should never be discouraged. Because, as we'll see, *doing the right thing* is the road to victory.

...ND MIND IN PERFECT HARMONY

> What I hear, I forget; What I see, I remember; What I do, I understand.
>
> Confucius, Chinese thinker and social philosopher (551–479 BC)[33]

From the brain's point of view, the body is no more than a big face, two giant hands and two big feet.[34] The brain uses fifty-something tiny facial muscles to communicate and build trust. It conducts our hands, the most perfect tools on earth, with a sensitivity and flexibility that's extremely hard to replicate artificially. And it controls the movements of our feet as we walk, run or jump, constantly correcting and adjusting to give us balance. What's in between is mainly for transportation, so kids are right when they start drawing humans: the brain is wired to think that we're tadpoles!

When we move our hands, take a walk or make faces, signals are sent to the brain, activating it. That's why people are better thinkers when they type on the computer, and that's why we doodle (or at least did in the past) when we're on the phone. In fact, this need to *do* in order to *think* was the founding idea behind LEGO Seriousplay: a strategy development methodology created by Johan Roos[35] and the toy producer LEGO.[36]

While we build the strategies or the competitive landscape physically, with our hands, the brain starts moving. Leonardo da Vinci wasn't sitting on his butt thinking. He was building, drawing, experimenting and playing around, because it's not the brain itself but its connectivity with the other parts of our body that makes us the most powerful technology on earth. For now. In *The Age of the Spiritual*

Machines: When Computers Exceed Human Intelligence[37] post-humanist Raymond Kurzweil claims that in 2029 we'll be able to acquire the power of 1000 human brains for as little as 1000 dollars. Even though one should apply a certain degree of skepticism to some of Kurtzweil's other ideas, the trend line proves his case in this matter – as do recent experiments like Watson.

NO MORE HUMAN DOMINATION?

> Unless there are slaves to do the ugly, horrible, uninteresting work, culture and contemplation become almost impossible. Human slavery is wrong, insecure, and demoralizing. On mechanical slavery, on the slavery of the machine, the future of the world depends.
>
> Oscar Wilde, Irish writer and poet (1854–1900)[38]

On June 16, 2010, IBM proudly announced that the producers of *Jeopardy!* had agreed to pitch the IBM supercomputer Watson against some of the game's best former players. Watson was well prepared. He was faster than thousands of ordinary desktop computers combined and had for three years been fed millions of documents from Wikipedia, making him able to answer almost any question. IBM had also tested Watson's capabilities in a series of matches against humans where he showed great expertise in several areas from cultural trivia to history and geography. He also performed well in sophisticated wordplay (*'Classic candy bar that's a female Supreme Court justice'* – *'What is Baby Ruth Ginsburg?'*).

What made IBM especially proud was neither that Watson won nor that the contestants started to think of Watson as human, calling him *he*. What made them proud was that Watson managed the human interaction and the game so well. Human interaction through speech is complex since the spoken language is so filled with nuances and ambiguity. For a computer to interpret and, more so, respond with a factual answer is extremely difficult. And unlike ordinary direct questions, *Jeopardy!* questions often include puns and subtlety, making them even harder to decipher. But Watson also handled those in a very human-like fashion.[39]

Pablo Picasso once said: *'Computers are useless. They can only give you answers.'*[40] Now we know that Picasso was wrong. They can raise questions too, and one of the greatest questions in the technological community is if or when a greater-than-human intelligence will be artificially created. Because even though processing power is now enough to sustain a thought-based economy, the knowledgeable man is still in charge.

THE CALL FOR THINKING

The most important contribution of management in the 20th century was to increase manual worker productivity fifty-fold. The most important contribution of management in the 21st century will be to increase knowledge worker productivity – hopefully by the same percentage.

Peter Drucker, Austrian management
consultant and writer (1909–2005)[41]

Search *knowledge worker productivity*, and you'll see that very few have gotten Drucker's message. Still, he was probably right (as he often was) and not too much ahead of his time. Throughout his lifelong career as a management thinker, regarded by many as the man who invented management, Drucker was often *just-in-time* with his comments on contemporary society and business. He set the course for others to follow, but was never so early that the audience missed the point.

In his bestseller from the mid-1990s, *The Cyberthief and the Samurai*,[42] Jeff Godell describes how *the samurai* hunted down Kevin Mitnick, the most skilled hacker of his time. After avoiding being caught by the FBI for more than two years, Mitnick made a mistake: he broke into the computer of one of America's most highly regarded IT-security experts Tsutomu Shimomura – son of the 2008 Nobel laureate in chemistry. In a couple of weeks Shimomura (together with computer journalist John Markoff) hunted down Mitnick and the FBI moved in. Mitnick spent five years in prison but is today a free man working as a computer security expert.[43]

Knowledge worker productivity is about solving inconvenient and unfamiliar problems efficiently, which both Shimomura and Mitnick are extremely good at. And that's what most of the people in the developed world will sooner or later be doing. In the world that Drucker is talking about it's obvious that productivity efforts must switch from operational productivity to intellectual productivity – or perhaps what we should call *thought productivity*. From driving as many screws per time unit to producing as many *Aha!*s per time unit as possible. And such a shift in focus will change the world order back to what it once was.

BACK TO BASICS

Now the reason the enlightened prince and the wise general conquer the enemy whenever they move and their achievements surpass those of ordinary men is foreknowledge.

Sun Tzu, Chinese military general, strategist
and philosopher (544–496 BC)[44]

In most developed economies around the world, 70 percent or more of the workforce is engaged in the service sector. In the USA this number is even higher: around 80 percent.[45] Most service workers are, more or less, knowledge workers, using their mental capacity to solve unfamiliar problems. And of those not active in the service sector, very few have unskilled jobs. In most developed countries the cadres of university graduates are approaching 50 percent of each class, and among 16–29 year olds expectations are even higher. In Europe and the USA around 70 percent have taken or are planning on taking a university degree, according to Kairos Future's *Global Youth Survey*.[46] As many as 12 percent are aiming for a PhD.

Simultaneously, China is moving away from being the factory floor of the world to instead become the hub of ideas and knowledge. To get there, it needs a population that is just as well-educated as that of the countries in the West. In many aspects China is already on its way. The country is the second-largest producer of scientific papers (after the USA) and, according to OECD's latest Pisa-reports, students from Shanghai are the best performing students in the world.[47] So even though they still might have a long way to go, China's ambition is set: it is on its way back to its historical position as the center of the earth. Back in the early 1800s, before the Opium Wars,[48] China accounted for one third of global GDP, and from a Chinese perspective the last 150 years have been a parenthesis, a deflection from the normal order.[49] There's just one unwanted (but probably temporary) obstacle to China's ambition to transform into a knowledge-based economy: the labor market isn't yet ready for the growing number of graduates leaving university each year.

LIFE IN THE ANTHILL

It's crowded at the top.

Anonymous

Before 2010, very few had heard about the Ant Tribes: China's young, well-educated but underpaid white-collar working-class, too poor to get a decent living, and definitely too poor to get married in a country where owning a home is a necessity for every man even thinking of getting married. After the launch of Lian's book[50] in September 2009, news started spreading and during 2010 a series of articles was published on this new social phenomenon in many parts of the world. According to Lian, these men are like ants because they are 'clever, weak and living in groups'.[51]

For two years, Lian led a team of more than 100 graduate students following the groups in university towns like Beijing, Shanghai, Guangzhou, Wuhan and Xi'an. Lian estimates the total population of the ant community in major cities across China to be about one million, with about 100,000 found in Beijing alone. Most of them are from poor rural families, and went to university with the hope of well-paid jobs. Having nothing to go back to, they struggle with temporary and low-paying jobs as insurance agents, electronic product sales representatives and waiters. In Beijing, members of the Ant Tribe are expected to earn just half the average income of 4000 yuan, and with rising rents they have to stay in cheap rooms in the outskirts of the mega-city, often without heating and not more than 10 square meters of space. This is not what they expected when they went to university, and not much to build a life on.

One such immigrant village is Tangjialing close to Beijing. Tangjialing originally had a population of 3000 but this has exploded to 50,000 with the influx of new Ant Tribe villagers. And what we are witnessing is probably just the beginning. More than six million graduates – half an age group – are expected to join the labor force each year (although most of them will not end up as members of the Ant Tribe). So clearly, some creative solutions are needed to provide for the rapidly growing Chinese middle class.

THE RETURN OF THE MEGA-PROJECT

Why make it small when you can make it big

For most cities in the world's emerging markets the needs are fundamental: housing and infrastructure such as transportation, water, sanitation and electricity. A while ago, Boston Consulting Group estimated that the required cumulative investment by 2030 is at the level of USD 30 to 40 trillion, the equivalent of 60 to 70 percent of the total global investment in infrastructure over the period. David Jin, BCG partner at the Shanghai office and co-author of the report says: 'The massive infrastructure-development needs across so many emerging-market cities dwarf anything that the world has seen before. A diverse set of global industries are being fundamentally reshaped by the demand that is now arising from this build-out, and many developed-market companies are missing out.'[52] It's hard not to believe him.

One of the countries with the greatest infrastructure needs is of course China. The country has been famous for having an investment-driven growth strategy, spending up to 40 percent of GDP on infrastructure investments, compared to less than 25 percent in India and far less in the West. For example, China is presently spending 11 percent of GDP on physical infrastructure, compared to 6 percent in India.[53] China is already into a giant railway investment wave, spending USD 1000 billion[54] on over 30,000 kilometers of new railways in the next five years, connecting all of its major cities with high-speed lines. So another multi-trillion dollar project to connect Europe with Central, East and Southeast Asia is perfectly in line with previous ambitions.

THE NEW ORIENT EXPRESS

With initial negotiations and surveys already complete, China is now making plans to connect its high speed rail line through 17 other countries in Asia and Eastern Europe in order to connect to the existing infrastructure in the EU.

Inhabitat weblog[55]

In March 2010 the above paragraph could be read on the Inhabitat website, the blog 'devoted to the future of design, tracking the innovations in technology, practices and materials that are pushing architecture and home design towards a smarter and more sustainable future'. Later that year, news surfaced major media across the world. On October 13, 2010 the *Telegraph* headlined: 'King's Cross to Beijing in two days on new high-speed rail network'.

At first glance it looks like another great ambition of the Chinese government – infamous for its sometimes exaggeratedly big thinking. But Wang Mengshu – a member of the Chinese Academy of Engineering and senior consultant on China's domestic high-speed rail project – claims that it wasn't China's idea to begin with. 'It was the other countries that came to us, especially India. These countries cannot fully implement the construction of a high-speed rail network and they hoped to draw on our experience and technology. ... We will use government money and bank loans, but the railways may also raise financing from the private sector and also from the host countries. We would actually prefer the other countries to pay in natural resources rather than make their own capital investment.'[56]

China already has the world's fastest train: the Harmony Express, which has a top speed of 350 km/h, running between Wuhan and Guangzhou. And since China is the most ambitious railway investor, it also possesses the most updated competence. In the fall of 2010, China officially opened its high-speed rail between Shanghai and Beijing – ahead of time. It was built with a construction pace of 40 kilometers a month, to be compared to the Citybanan project in Stockholm (albeit tunneling through and between the most fragile of the islands that constitute my capital) which at the moment advances by 60 *meters* a month.[57] The pace illustrates an ambition (which may, in the case of the high-speed rail, have gone too fast, considering the technical and other problems that followed the opening) that is shown in other areas too. While foreign students at Stockholm University are temporarily housed in tents at the start of each school year because the municipality can't provide enough student apartments, the Chinese would probably just build a city for them.

ROOM FOR THE NEW METROPOLITANS

In the past we went to the unspoiled land for opportunities. Now we head for the cites.

In 2005 Alejandro Gutierrez of the engineering and design giant Arup got a strange message from Hong Kong. On the line were some McKinsey consultants who were putting together a business plan for the Shanghai Industrial Investment Corporation. Their client wanted to transform a small island in the outskirts of Shanghai into a 500,000-inhabitant city. The only problem was that the marshy Eastern tip of the massive, mostly undeveloped island was the major migratory stop for one of the rarest birds in the world: the black-faced spoonbill. Would it be possible to bring business to the island without messing up the bird habitat, McKinsey wondered, knowing that Gutierrez's firm were specialists on big-city design projects and that Gutierrez was a young and rising star at Arup's London headquarters.[58]

The rest isn't yet history. It's future, because the zero-emission city of Dongtan at the mouth of Yangtze River hasn't yet been built. According to the plan, the city should have been ready for the first 10,000 inhabitants to move in for Shanghai Expo 2010. This never happened due (according to the media) to greed and bureaucracy combined with shortcomings in technology. But still, Dongtan is a brilliant example not only of the high ambitions of the Chinese government and business leaders, but also of probably the largest investment area for the next 20 years, and the greatest opportunity to fight climate change.

Over the next 20 years, migration and urbanization will continue to grow in developing countries such as China,

India, Nigeria, Mexico and Brazil. Predictions indicate that in emerging markets, city dwellers will go from 2.3 to 3.5 billion until 2030,[59] and primarily to cities of Dongtan's size. By contrast, cities in developed markets will only grow by 100 million over the same time period. But this means opportunities too. If we manage to build cities just half as good as the ambitious Dongtan project, we would be able to improve both living conditions and climate conditions at the same time.

BUILD YOUR DREAMS

If you want to change an industry, being first is a good idea.

From the end of the Cultural Revolution in the late 1970s until today, China's share of global GDP has risen from 4 to 15 percent (2003) and is estimated to be 23 percent by 2030,[60] changing the country's role not only in trade and economics but also in geopolitics. China is now the world's leading car and luxury-product market, and also its number one emitter of greenhouse gases. However, it's obvious that the country's ambitions are strong in future-critical areas such as infrastructure and cleantech too. In Dongtan and its three sister cities planned for, the ambition was to build a city with zero-greenhouse-emission transit and complete self-sufficiency in water and energy, together with the use of zero-energy building principles. The only vehicles allowed in Dongtan would be powered by electricity or hydrogen – a field still waiting for revolution.

The Chinese battery manufacturer Build Your Dreams (BYD) attempts to be the first to put a mass-produced electric vehicle on the market. Compared to most auto manufacturers, BYD is a newcomer. It was founded in the mid 1990s but has reached the top of battery making in less than 15 years, today being the leading supplier of batteries to Nokia, Samsung and Motorola. Most experts have for years assumed that whichever auto manufacturer first develops a battery powerful enough to run its cars will also be the first with a reliable car, and one of those believing that BYD might be that company is Warren Buffet, philanthropist and the world's second-richest man. Buffet has a long-term perspective on investments and is normally right (that's why he is so rich!) and in 2008 he threw in more than USD 200 million to get 10 percent of BYD.[61] So, will it be BYD, Tata or a more well-known Japanese, US or European automaker that builds our dreams of a carbon-free car tomorrow?

THE RACE TOWARDS THE FUTURE

You could fight the battle over and over again. And still not win.

Going from battery manufacture to auto-making is a leap almost unfeasible for most companies. Just to get to the starting line, BYD has had to embrace a completely new business model that's taken them from invisible subcontractor to a maker of branded products, now ready to challenge the global giants. And they're not alone. Hundreds, if not thousands of Chinese companies are at the moment diversifying their business models and moving from components and subcontracting to branded goods and services, making life hard for companies such as Swedish telecom giant Ericsson, which has to fight fiercely with relative newcomers such as Huawei and ZTE.[62]

Showing presence and ambition is important in winning attractive Chinese contracts, so in 1997 Ericsson inaugurated its first software research and development facility in Shanghai, where the staff of 900 engineers constitutes an integral part of Ericsson's global R&D network.[63] In 2009 Ericsson planned on hiring 1000 new researchers as a part of their strategy to win a bigger share of the country's third-generation telecom market.[64] This is a battle of life and death. Almost 20 years ago Richard d'Aveni, Professor of Strategic Management, named the new competitive landscape *hypercompetition*. Since then, he has been dedicated to understanding and describing the rapidly changing globalized thought economy. D'Aveni's research shows that very few make it over time and that within-industry heterogeneity in performance has risen dramatically over the last 15 years.[65]

Ericsson isn't the only company to have realized the value of doing market research specifically for China. As it has become the largest market for many industries, China is attracting more and more research labs from large multinationals. China has the largest Internet population and is the biggest market for desktop computers, so consequently Intel has a research lab in Beijing for semiconductors and server networks. China is the largest auto market, so General Motors, Volkswagen and others have large and growing auto research centers across the country.[66] But as competition grows fiercer, it is export-oriented companies like Huawei that are positioned to become market leaders.

HOW CHEAP IS CHEAP?

I will build a car for the great multitude. It will be large enough for the family, but small enough for the individual to run and care for. It will be constructed of the best materials, by the best men to be hired, after the simplest designs that modern engineering can devise. But it will be so low in price that no man making a good salary will be unable to own one – and enjoy with his family the blessing of hours of pleasure in God's great open spaces.

Henry Ford, US industrialist and founder of
Ford Motor Company (1863–1947)[67]

In 2007, the question 'How cheap is cheap?' was raised by Bloomberg Businessweek in an article featuring the future of the automotive industry. The background was a statement by Renault-Nissan Chief Executive Carlos Ghosn at a plant-opening ceremony in India 2010. Ghosn's qualified guess was that, for cars, the magic number was USD 3000. In the same ceremony Ghosn declared that Renault-Nissan was already taking up the next challenge: a model with a price as low as USD 2500. With that, Renault-Nissan was the first global automaker to take up competition with new ambitious players such as Tata Motors and its Tata Nano. But how cheap is USD 3000 really? Everything is relative of course, but it's definitely cheap. In comparison, Henry Ford's Model T of 1909 standard cost USD 850 (equivalent to USD 20,500 today), while most competitor products at the time came at USD 2000–3000. In 1930 there were already 23 million cars in the US or almost one in every household, which is remarkable even though the price of a Model T Ford had fallen by 1926 to USD 295.[68]

The growing markets in the developing world are forcing companies to think globally, and there's no doubt that while we're heading towards much more comfortable, secure and reliable cars at a tenth of the standard car price 100 years ago, a car costing USD 2500 in today's money will be available to a large proportion of the world population. But what else does it mean that India, China and a few others are starting a race to the bottom in the automaker industry? A great deal, because just as Ford's revolutionary ambitions to produce cars for his workers sparked a cascade of improvements, so will the ambitions of Tata, Renault-Nissan and others. The reason is simple. When you intend to cut the price to a half, a third or even a quarter, you can't just strip the vehicle of a number of functions. Instead, you need to rethink the whole manufacturing and distribution process, and eventually that rethinking will change the industry.

THE BOTTOM IS THE NEW TOP

> There is one thing stronger than all the armies in the world; and that is an idea whose time has come.
>
> Victor Hugo, French writer, statesman
> and activist (1802–85)[69]

A hundred years ago, Henry Ford revolutionized the West by not only producing the first really affordable car, but also by introducing a new way of treating employees. And he wasn't the only industrialist with welfare ambitions at that time. My mother's grandfather was offered a job at pulp-and-paper company Mo & Domsjö's production plant at Norrbyskär, a tiny island in the Gulf of Bothnia archipelago in the north of Sweden. By creating an ideal society for the workers and their families – including pensions, social security and free housing with electric lights – the head and owner of the company, Frans Kempe, became a role model for a new and more humane society where people get decent pay, a good education and access to health care. To my family it was almost like winning the lottery. My grandmother's oldest brother, a good scholar, was rapidly identified as gifted, and ended up as head of engineering at Mo & Domsjö. Being a caring person, he made sure that all of his younger siblings received university educations as well – all but my own grandmother, who (according to her closest brother) was 'intelligent but lazy' and married instead of going to university.

Henry Ford, Frans Kempe and their peers focused on the masses of the West, the *then* future middle class: the people that were about to receive their political voice, leaving farming behind and moving to metropolitan areas, becoming blue- and white-collar workers. Today, the Henry Fords of the 21st century are likewise focusing on the present and future global middle class, in BRIC[70] or CIVETS[71] countries, but also in other parts of the world, such as the rapidly growing East Africa – a region where reality is often far from the pictures that we're fed through the TV screen. Because, as we're about to find out, change doesn't necessarily come from the West any more.

NO MORE TRICKLE DOWN

What the rich do today, the masses will do tomorrow.
Traditional view of diffusion of
ideas and behaviors

When French dairy producer Danone launched its joint venture with microfinance pioneer Grameen Bank in Bangladesh the plan was to build local micro plants with the production capacity of one hundredth of a normal yogurt facility, partly because of a lack of refrigerating capacity. What wasn't in the plan was that these factories would be almost as efficient as the larger ones. 'It has inspired a plant in Indonesia, which we've already built. Now we're talking about other business markets where the plant could be adopted', says Emmanuel Marchant at Danone in an interview with FastCompany.[72]

The Danone case illustrates that everything we've ever known about innovation, namely that innovation *trickles down* (rich people getting the new gadgets first while the rest of the world gets our castoffs as markets reach scale and prices come down), may not be the only truth. The traditional model of the diffusion of innovation is if not fully replaced at least complemented by the opposite model: trickle-up innovation. McKinsey (who has conducted a large study in the field) summarizes the drivers behind the phenomenon in four bullets:

- Developing markets have low-cost, high-quality workers who can both create and execute great ideas;

- These markets have hard-to-reach consumers who force companies to come up with new ways to serve them;

- Emerging-market consumers don't want Western retreads but their own unique products and services, some of which may also appeal to Westerners; and

- There are suppliers in developing markets who are rapidly accessing developed markets.[73]

One example of potential trickle-up is Finnish telecom giant Nokia's ambition to use Kenya as the first market for a service that lets people shop using voice commands to browse for goods. The choice is natural. Nokia has for years seen growth from developing countries, so why not start developing where growth arises? Of course, everything won't trickle up. Nokia isn't sure whether any services launched in developing countries will ever reach the West. But the experiences from innovation in and for the developing world will definitely have a huge impact on the products and services we get in the developed world.

THE END OF LOCAL

A top world medical destination with excellent service and superior value.

Bumrungrad International Hospital's slogan[74]

Google Bumrungrad and you'll find hotel offers and references to a hospital. Why? Because Bumrungrad since the late 1990s *is* medical tourism, and hotels in its surroundings in Bangkok are prospering thanks to the hospital. With representation offices in 21 locations in Asia, Africa and Europe, and with 1.2 million patients coming in from 200 countries across the globe every year, Bumrungrad International Hospital is Southeast Asia's largest private medical center. Its services range from comprehensive checkups to cardiac surgery, and as a modern, service-oriented hospital, Bumrungrad doesn't just have lobby worthy a five-star hotel. It's also present on Facebook and Twitter.

The hospital combines international high-quality service with reasonable costs, making it appealing to people from different regions. Bumrungrad yearly welcomes around 30,000 patients from both Europe and the USA, 100,000 from the Middle East, and growing numbers from Africa and Australia. From the USA, patients come for prices that are normally 50–80 percent lower than those at home, which for patients with no or poor insurance makes all the difference. For Europeans it's the direct access to care that attracts. A patient may have been in pain, waiting for eight months to get a knee replacement. At Bumrungrad she can get the surgery right away.

However, Bumrungrad didn't become international only by intention. The opportunity was created in part when the baht was depreciated by 50 percent due to the financial crisis at the end of the 1990s. While large loans in dollars were a heavy burden and brought Bumrungrad close to bankruptcy, international patients paying in dollars or dollar-linked currencies suddenly found their services very cheap. Bumrungrad, which in Thai means *care for the people*, is listed on the Thai stock-exchange with an annual turnover of USD 260 million, and is expanding its operation internationally through subsidiaries and management deals with other hospitals. So Bumrungrad International Hospital is indeed a living example that not even healthcare is local anymore – a movement seen not least in politics.[75]

THE POWER OF POLITICS

In the global village, politics – 'the affairs of the city' – goes global.

In January 2010, Mark R. Pinto of Santa Clara-based Applied Materials became the first chief technology officer of a major US technology company to move to China. And Applied Materials isn't just any company: it's the world's biggest supplier of equipment used to make semiconductors, solar panels and flat-panel displays. Today, China produces two thirds of the world's solar panels. 'President Obama has often spoken about creating clean-energy jobs in the United States. But China has shown the political will to do so', Pinto says in an interview.[76] And indeed, political will and action is becoming increasingly important. While in the West the market has been in charge for most of the 1900s and definitely so during the most recent decades, politics has slowly begun to re-inaugurate itself through, for instance, environmental issues. And if Mr Pinto is right, China might actually come to lead the battle for a greener world.

Like many other things in our world, the attitude towards politics seems to be cyclical. Because these cycles are about 80 years long people are now looking for a strong leader, just as they were in the 1930s. (We will return to this in Chapter 7.) But there's one big difference between politics now and then.[77] Politics today operates on a much higher systemic level through multilateral treaties – not to mention the now 27-member European Union where 17 of the members even share currencies, inflation targets and monetary policy. At the time of the Swedish EU-membership referendum in 1994, one of the biggest discussion topics was the regulation regarding the size and the shape of cucumbers that would be imposed if Sweden were to join the union. Today, following the 2008 and 2011 financial crises, the common concerns are related to PIGS – Portugal, Italy, Greece and Spain – and to recent institutional change, such as the Basel III agreement that regulates banking even in non-euro countries like the UK or Sweden. But the picture is clearing: issues regarding global finances or global warming can't be handled country by country. They require the cooperation and coordination of billions, which in turn also raises the need for strong leaders to guide the process.

It seems that de Gaulle was right when he concluded that politics are too serious a matter to be left to politicians. In order to fix problems in Greece and Italy the two countries' elected politicians were replaced by internationally well-respected technocrats in the fall of 2011: Lucas Papademos and Mario Monti. The story continues.

47

2

A NEW PARADIGM EMERGING

We see what we're trained to see. So how do
you see what you've never seen before?

Let's start by reflecting for a moment on the cascade of
images and examples given in the previous chapter. What
do they tell us about business and society in the early 2000s?
Are we, as I strongly believe, heading towards a new world
that is in many (but far from all) aspects *qualitatively* different? And if so, will the shift be sudden, rapid and dramatic,
or a smooth turning with which we won't realize what has
happened until it already has? If I were a betting man, I'd
bet on the latter.

In Table 2.1, some of the aspects discussed are summarized in the format of *from–to*, and in this case, from what
I've called the Old World to the New World. The table summarizes most of what has been discussed so far, from truly
paradigmatic shifts to areas where the change is a more
incremental part of a long-term process. Some of the shifts
have already almost taken place while others have hardly
started and, of course, most industries and companies are
living in both worlds simultaneously. There are rarely defi-
nite *either–ors*, but the point is that we are heading from
left to right in Table 2.1, from the Old World into an as-yet
only partly known New World.

Table 2.1 The paradigm shift from the Old World to the New World

INFORMATION AND THINKING	OLD WORLD	NEW WORLD
ANALYTICS:	Focus on figures	Focus on patterns
INFORMATION:	In silos	In networks or pools
ANALYTICS APPLIED TO:	Small numbers (samples), occasionally	Large numbers (total populations), constantly
SCIENTIFIC PARADIGM:	Understand *why* it works	Understand *what* works
KNOWING AND DOING:	Know and you'll do	Do and you'll know
THINKING IS:	Inner reflection	Interplay between reflection and action

GEOPOLITICS	OLD WORLD	NEW WORLD
GEOPOLITICAL PARADIGM:	US-centric world	Multi-centric world
THE HOME OF MEGA-PROJECTS:	USA	China
CHINA'S ROLE:	Production hub	Ideas and knowledge hub
DEVELOPING COUNTRIES ARE, FROM A DEVELOPED-WORLD PERSPECTIVE:	Poor and problematic	Interesting markets that set new standards and challenge incumbent market players
AFRICA IS:	The land of hopelessness and despair	The land of the future
INVESTMENTS FLOW:	From North to …	From South to South
POLITICS:	Retreating and deregulating the national level	Advancing and reregulating on the supra-national level

(continued)

Table 2.1 Continued

CONSUMERS AND CONSUMER MARKETS	OLD WORLD	NEW WORLD
CONSUMER PRODUCT INNOVATION DRIVEN BY:	Adding new features for the global upper class	Products cheap enough for the global middle class
CONSUMERS MARKETS IN FOCUS:	The Western middle class	The global middle class
PRIME CUSTOMER VALUE:	Excellent functions	Experiences, transformation and togetherness
BRANDS ARE CONTROLLED BY:	Brand owners	Consumers and employees

INNOVATION	OLD WORLD	NEW WORLD
TECHNOLOGY:	Investments, machines	Usage, software
INNOVATION STARTS WITH:	Technology	End users
INNOVATIONS IN FOCUS:	Products and services	Business concepts and models
INNOVATION IS:	Breakthrough thinking	Experiments and evolutionary approach
INNOVATION TAKES PLACE:	In R&D departments	In interaction with partners, customers and others
TECHNOLOGY INVESTMENTS FOCUSED ON:	Hardware	Software
INVESTMENT FOCUS AND BUSINESS OPPORTUNITIES:	(Automobile and) IT-infrastructure	Greentech and green infrastructure

ORGANIZATIONS AND PERFORMANCE	OLD WORLD	NEW WORLD
BUSINESS CONTEXT:	Fairly stable	Fairly turbulent
PRIME TEMPORAL FOCUS:	Mid-term (planning)	Now and for ever (long-term)
BUSINESS RISKS:	Low or medium	High (and often reputational)
CORPORATE COMPETITIVE ADVANTAGE BUILT ON:	Excellent production	Superior thinking
CEO TOP PRIORITY:	Operational productivity	Innovation and thought productivity
RELATION TO THE EXTERNAL WORLD:	Secluding, secretive	Inclusive, open, transparent (but sometimes opaque)
OVERALL STRATEGY:	Inside-out	Outside-in
PRODUCTIVITY FOCUS:	Worker productivity	Knowledge/thought productivity
WORK IS ABOUT:	Pay	Fun and personal development
EMPLOYEE COMMITMENT DRIVEN BY:	Loyalty	Challenges and goal-oriented team work
BUSINESS IS:	Company-centric	Customer-centric
KEY PERSON IN THE COMPANY:	COO (Chief Operating Officer)	CCA (Chief Corporate Analyst)
KPI-FOCUS:	Ends – are we *delivering* what we said?	Processes – are we *doing* what we need to do?

Looking at Table 2.1 you'll probably think that many of the trends are soon to level off. Let's take social media as an example. Wikipedia started in 2001, Facebook technically in 2004 but in reality a few years later. Since more or less everyone[1] already has Facebook or LinkedIn accounts, it's easy to believe that the social media revolution has already happened. However, nothing could be more wrong. A completely different but in my opinion more correct interpretation would be to say that the world of social media is where e-mail was in the late 1990s, which means still at an early stage. So if mine is the correct interpretation, what does it mean to your business? And what will it mean in 1, 3, 5 or 10 years time?

And what if China *really* will transform from being the world's factory, passing through a position as the leading consumer market (where it partly already is, in terms of sales of cars, luxury goods, computers and so on) to becoming the knowledge hotspot of the world? What if it becomes a global supplier of branded low-cost, high-quality goods and services? And what if India follows that same path (although starting with services, not production)? What if it is a process rather than a great leap, which means that *the future* isn't evenly distributed, but happens earlier in certain industries and sectors and later in others? And what if that process is two, three or maybe even four times faster now than when South Korea went from being one of the poorest countries in the world in the early 1960s to becoming one of the richest and most developed today? And what if...?

A COMPLEX WORLD

Whichever way we choose to make a proper description of the core drivers of global change, we end up in the same overall consequence: *complexity*. A very straightforward effect of complexity is that the organizational survival rate over time declines. It's simply much harder to survive today than it used to be. A McKinsey study ten years ago showed that in the 1920s and 1930s, the average lifetime of a Standard & Poor 500 company was 60–70 years. Today it's 15.[2] So if you don't keep up with the innovation rate in your market you'll be beaten and eaten.

With a more complex business landscape, more relations, larger markets and remote competition from below, most companies are trying to adapt and compete by new means. These include closer customer adaptation, open innovation, outsourcing of non-critical functions, integrated solutions, business model innovation, and broadened and more varied product portfolios. This results in more complex businesses, which requires more flexible, or should we say more complex organizations. A rough sketch of what faces most organizations in today's world is shown in Figure 2.1.

Another stream of external complexity comes from the supply and employee sides of the business landscape. Regardless of whether a company is active on a domestic or international market, employee complexity tends to grow too with rising education level and more diversified job

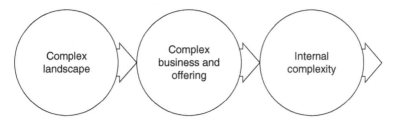

Figure 2.1   External complexity induces internal complexity

expectations. The ambition to outsource less critical functions reduces internal transaction costs and some aspects of internal complexity, but as a consequence the company's external complexity increases instead, generating external uncertainties and transaction costs.

Simplified complexity

If we define the complexity of a system as the number of possible configurations of that system (that is, the number of shapes it can take) it's easy to argue, as we have seen, that in at least in some parts of the world most industries and even nations are more complex than before. Complexity will increase exponentially with the number of new factors that have to be considered in the decision-making process. As the number of external contacts increases and your product portfolio and customer pool diversifies, the more decisions you have to make and the more complex your decision-making process will become. If we also take into consideration the fact that the rate of change at least up until now is accelerating, the number of *possible reconfigurations* over a specific time period is growing at an ever higher rate. Table 2.2 illustrates the four levels of complexity for the external business context.

However, from a managerial point of view, complexity isn't just the number of configurations, scenarios or alternatives that one has to manage or choose between. It's actually much simpler than this. Normally, the real degree of complexity is just the number of issues one has to deal with at the moment. As long as the uncertainty of each issue or trend is low, complexity increases only linearly with the growing number of issues. Thus, scenario planning and trend analysis help you in keep it simple (but not too simple).

Table 2.2 The four levels of external complexity

COMPLEXITY LEVEL	CHARACTERISTIC
FIRST	*Number* of *issues* or trends that need to be considered
SECOND	*Change* in the number of issues that need to be considered
THIRD	Number of possible *outcomes* of the issues that have to be considered
FOURTH	*Change* in the outcomes of the issues that have to be considered

BUILDING THE JAMMING ORGANIZATION

Successful companies survive complex environments by managing the crucial balance between flexibility and structure. Ever since the first modern theories on strategy were introduced in the 1960s, the alignment between an organization and its context has been the number one principle. This principle goes back to systems theory, which claims that in order to manage a system you need to be at least as diverse (or complex) as the system that you're managing. Consider a football match and you understand what the principle means. In order to win you need to have more flexible, varied and hopefully unpredictable play than your competitor. This principle is often called *Ashby's law of requisite variety*.[3]

But like every football lover, player and coach knows: you can't prepare for everything. You need to have a system to follow. One of the reasons for this is that we have limited mental (or managerial) bandwidth. A popular version of the limitations of the mental bandwidth, sometimes called *Miller's law*, says that the span is seven – which would explain why seven is the holiest number in many cultures, why there are seven days in a week and so forth.[4] Alignment requires complexity, while managerial function requires simplicity. So Ashby versus Miller is the challenge ahead.

Being a fighter pilot

The United States Air Force assesses a fighter pilot's ability with the OODA Loop: the cycle of Observation (sensing environmental signals), Orientation (interpreting), Decision (selection from a repertoire of responses) and Action (executing a response). Pilots with faster OODA Loops tend to win dogfights, while those with slower ones get more parachute practice. Speed is the critical factor.[5]

Speed is also important in management. But it's not enough. Successful managers of turbulent business environments need to be like fighter pilots; they need to be speedy and be able to improvise. But they also need to be able to rely on structure and pace. They need a systematic approach to scanning the business environment and turning insights into strategy and action. The framework on which most of what we do at Kairos Future is based is called TAIDA. This is a scenario-planning loop consisting of five phases: Tracking, Analyzing, Imaging, Deciding and Acting.[6]

Just like fighter pilots, successful managers try to understand what happens in the outside world and plot their way into the future through systematic experimentation. Discipline, routines, rules of thumb and analytics provide them with a set of actions from which to choose, while the actual moment of truth often also requires quite a bit of creativity, playfulness and risk-taking as the future never meets our expectations perfectly. So companies should learn from the US Air Force how to link the understanding of the future with ideas and strategic moves that help them survive.

Thinking, playing and gardening

Continuing the path of metaphors, the overall conclusion of this book is that companies need to be more like jam sessions. A well-tuned band, whose members are used to playing together, easily combines the stable foundation of a thought-out, metronomic and harmonious accompaniment on which the flexibility of some playful and unexpected improvisation can be built. They know how to balance discipline with creativity, and speedy decision-making with endurance. If you add to the accompaniment and improvisation a third dimension that nurtures the conditions under which thinking and playing are at their best – a good manager for an example – you'll get the foundations of the jamming organization illustrated in Figure 2.2.

First, the thinking dimension concerns creating the future through mental exploration. It requires systematic planning, procedures, decisive management and participation to set up structures that support innovation processes over the whole timeline, from alternative thinking and possibility scanning to implementation. Next, the playing dimension is the action-oriented, improvisational supplement to thinking, based in exploration of the future through creating it. Experience, strategic experimentation, adaptivity and independence are the core capabilities behind speed and evolutionary renewal, and require a type of management that is inspiring, provocative, innovative and visionary. Finally, the gardening dimension nurtures

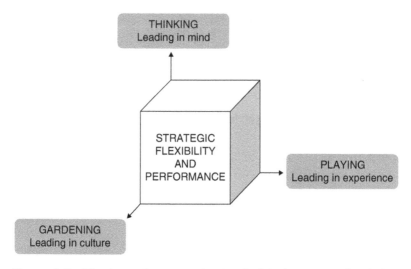

Figure 2.2 The jamming organization behind strategic flexibility and performance

the other two by designing the organizational prerequisites for the future to happen. Tailoring a controlled culture of openness, ambition, creativity and team spirit requires a leadership that is empowering, that listens and that invigorates the strategic conversation on a day-to-day basis.

The dynamic position of a jamming organization will have to be re-conquered over and over again through tuning, rehearsing and learning new pieces, but the performance created when thinking, playing and gardening harmonize is definitely worth fighting for. However, all three dimensions need to be equally strong in order for the company to be healthy. If thinking becomes too heavy, the firm risks ending up in the analysis trap: a frustrating situation of being stuck on the starting blocks. If, on the other hand, playing gets too much attention, the business ends up in an entrepreneurial trap in which it changes things just for the sake of change – renewal that introduces too much risk into operations. Too much of a gardening approach instead leads to the impossible project of building the perfect organization, which takes far too much attention away from the parts that are generating money. Obviously, if all three are weak or lacking, the company will stagnate or even die.

CHOOSING PERSPECTIVES

In the final chapter of this book, you'll find a hands-on guide for how to build a jamming organization of your own. The first step, however, is to decide what paradigm, what world perception and philosophy to lean on, follow and have as your working hypothesis through this process. The reason for this is simple: it's very hard to be consistent and decisive with too much *both–and* thinking. And choosing a perspective on how the world works and *what* works in business is exactly what football coach Nanne Bergstrand, Fujitsu's marketers, Procter & Gamble's A. G Lafley, Steve Jobs, Hans Rosling, Floatingsheep, Husqvarna, James and Benjamin Haywood, Lego, Anton Abele, Jessica Jackley and Matt Flannery, Wang Chuanfu, Applied Materials, Bumrungrad International, Dave Carrol, and others in the examples above did.

If, like me, you believe that there's some sense in the idea that the world at large and the world of business is moving from Old to New, and that this transition will probably fundamentally change the conditions for most businesses, then it's probably worth reading the following chapters. If not, you can stop now because next I am going to summarize the concept of the Thought economy, which is a fundamental part of this transition. After that, we'll take a look at what research tells us about how to surf trends into the New World.

3

THE THOUGHT ECONOMY

The future is like a stray dog, whoever catches it gets it.

The big consequence of the megatrends and changes that we have seen in the previous chapters is the emergence of a new economy. The Old World that we're leaving has been called by most the industrial society. We've named it that for decades, and for good reasons. Its production base was made up of industry, and although a minority of the working population worked in that industry, most in one way or another relied on it. But those times are history. From both an economical perspective and a general global and geopolitical point of view, society is now moving into a new phase, a new era. Many before me have said the same, and today's society has already been given many names. To name a few:

- Network society (Castells)[1]

- Service economy (Fuchs, Gershuny)[2]

- Information society, economy or age (Masuda, Hawken)[3]

- Risk society (Beck, Giddens)[4]

- Post-industrial society (Bell)[5]

- Post-Fordism society (Amim)[6]

- Third wave (Toffler)[7]

- Dream society (Jensen)[8]

- Experience economy (Pine & Gilmore)[9]

- Knowledge economy (Drucker)[10].

I have chosen to proceed with a somewhat different terminology, however. From here on, I will refer to this new era as the Thought economy or T-economy because it is first and foremost an economic system in which competitive power is based on thinking: the ability to produce as many powerful concepts as possible. While the traditional means of production according to economic theory are labor, capital, raw materials and (sometimes) technology, the T-economy introduces a new resource into the equation. This new production factor comes in the form of information, patents, ideas and other products created and exploited by the power of human thought (hence the Thought economy). In this chapter I will introduce new principles for the successful management of markets and organizations in the T-economy. I will start with some general ideas (partly provided in my previous book *Scenario Planning*[11]), and then continue with the hands-on principles.

THOUGHT-CELLS AND THOUGHT-NETS

Figure 3.1 shows schematically how different production eras have evolved and leveled off over the past 1000 years or so. The raw material based society evolved from local more or less self-reliant societies to global colonial trading economies, while the industrial society has more recently

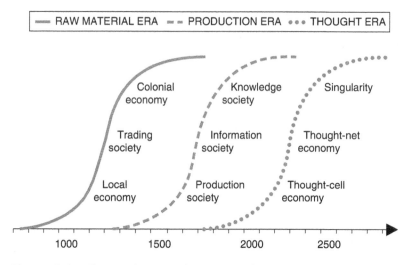

RAW MATERIAL ERA — — PRODUCTION ERA ••• THOUGHT ERA

Colonial economy

Knowledge society

Singularity

Trading society

Information society

Thought-net economy

Local economy

Production society

Thought-cell economy

1000   1500   2000   2500

Figure 3.1 The evolution of societies, from raw material era to thought era

turned from a relatively simple production economy into the 20th-century information society. However, another major shift is already taking place, thanks to the technological progress of former eras. Instead of acting just as muscle enhancers, technoloy is now becoming intelligent slaves, performing ever more qualified activities as the singularity is drawing nearer – the theoretical milestone where intelligence greater than human intelligence can be artificially created.

In short, creating value in the industrial economy was about turning raw material (and manpower) into sellable (and often undifferentiated) products as efficiently as possible. This meant that the those in possession of the most efficient factories were the winners of the game. In Figure 3.2, the second layer illustrates the core parts of the value chain of the industrial economy. In the now emerging T-economy, however, the value-chain consists of three layers instead of one,

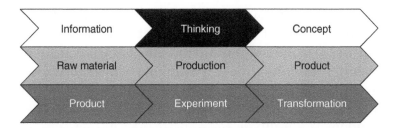

Information	Thinking	Concept
Raw material	Production	Product
Product	Experiment	Transformation

Figure 3.2 The three-level Thought-net and its Thought-cell (in black)

and the key to understanding this economy is the notion of Thought-cells and Thought-nets. In this new economy, information (or patents, ideas and so forth) is the new raw material. It's out there – sometimes for free and sometimes for purchase – but always available and ready to roll.

In the T-economy, thinking is the new critical production factor, and Thought-cells, turning information and ideas into viable concepts, are the new factories. These concepts then serve as a traditional production factor in the middle layer, where they are the core components in the production of valuable products and services. The middle layer is what the industrial society used to be about, but can now be regarded as primarily an add-on to its research and innovation activities. Finally, its output – the product or service – is nothing more than raw material in the value creating process where customers assisted by those products, create meaning, development, value. When customers experiment or play around with products or services they will hopefully find themselves transforming into something better. If not, they will not purchase the products. This me-making transformation can be used as part of the input to the top layer. By including the environment and allowing open innovation, the three levels form a Thought-net.

The winner of the game is the company with the strongest combined power of their Thought-net and Thought-cell.

In the T-economy, production efficiency is a secondary capability, as thoughts and thinking will diversify markets and products enough to create semi-protected niches for firms with good thinking. Apple's journey during the 2000s is a brilliant example of this. But what *is* good thinking according to customers? Well, what our studies have shown is that – along with the emergence of the Thought economy – we are witnessing the materialization of an experience-driven transformation society in which customers (both consumers and B2B customers) and the workforce constantly seek transformation and experience. This means that the company with the best me-making capabilities (that is, the company that succeeds in offering its customers and employees self-fulfillment, transformation and togetherness[12]) is the one to which customers and employees will turn. What companies need to do, therefore, is remake themselves into a combination of Thought-cells and Thought-nets where all the stakeholders are involved in recreating the company, and so making it a better version of itself.

Companies like Apple, Google, Procter & Gamble and others that know how to collect (i.e. buy or borrow) ideas and information, and understand how to turn them into concepts that fulfill dreams are the winners of the T-game. However, Apple wouldn't be Apple if it didn't know that products are nothing more than raw material in the lives of the consumers. The value of a product or service – to an end consumer as well as an industrial buyer – lies in the product's ability to transform the buyer, to make them a better version of themselves. Therefore, bringing buyers and the employees into the Thinking process by creating a Thought-net, as Procter & Gamble, Lego, Starbucks[13] and others have done, is another critical factor in success.

THE CRY FOR THOUGHT LEADERSHIP

Finally, what does this new era mean to leadership? What does it mean that leaders need to be more like thought leaders and apply more innovative and visionary leadership? From an employee perspective, leadership could be divided into five dimensions:

- **Empowering**. Authorizing and encouraging. Coaches people to take responsibility here and now, to find their own way and to set their own goals.

- **Listening**. Attentive and empathetic. A mentor that is prepared to step aside for a while to give room for new talents to show their skill.

- **Decisive**. Fearless and non-political. Makes tough decisions when necessary, even though it might hurt the leader themselves.

- **Innovative**. Creative and thought-provoking. Leads innovation, experimentation and renewal both in daily work and on bigger issues.

- **Visionary**. Forward-oriented and inspiring. Shows where to go, has great plans for the future and refuses to be let down by current problems.

Leaders are different. Some are more listening while others are more provocative. Some are visionary, others empowering. The style differs from person to person, and from culture to culture. In general, though, managers in mature markets such as Europe and North America are more into empowerment, listening and decisive leadership, whereas managers from emerging markets are more visionary, innovative, forward-oriented and thought-provoking. So what makes a successful leadership style? Well, it depends. It depends on whether you want to make people happy, build trust and confidence, or increase commitment and motivation. If we look at how the dimensions are related to each other, to some extent empowering leadership seems to be the opposite of the decisive and visionary kind. Similarly, listening leadership is to some extent the opposite of innovative leadership, at least in terms of everyday innovation and improvement. Innovative leadership fosters inspiration, empowering leadership is the driver of appreciation and empowerment, and visionary goal-setting leadership is best aimed at creating a collaborating and development-oriented work culture.

One of our own international studies shows that leaders in most companies are strongest in the empowering dimension: on average, four out of five employees consider their leaders empowering. The weakest areas are the thought leadership styles: innovative and visionary leadership. These styles may be less important to making people satisfied at work than for instance the listening style, but in today's relentlessly changing business landscape they are crucial to long-term success. And thought leadership and change isn't something just for managers and leaders. It's a challenge for everyone.

FIVE PRINCIPLES FOR SUCCESSFUL MANAGEMENT

Thought as a leadership practice and virtue is necessary for success in the T-economy, but it's not enough. More than anything excellence is a based on habits, practices and organizational behaviors. So how do we ensure that we have the most adequate behaviors for the coming T-economy?

A few years ago, we were asked to help *futurize* a global ICT company's employee survey so that it would measure future success factors rather than simple employee satisfaction. After thorough research, beginning with a scenario analysis of the future of the ICT industry so as to understand the future corporate context, and a desk-study of recent management research (our own and others'), a model for future organizational capabilities – the Future Capital Index – was developed and operationalized. In order to determine the prime performance drivers, all managers were asked to evaluate their units' performance compared to competitors in the same market. To get a more objective analysis of performance, customer satisfaction data was integrated in the evaluation process, and a reference study was conducted in the company's major markets.

The results of the company's first yearly survey were brought into its new vision and overall corporate guidelines and principles, and also taken into consideration when developing the leadership framework and other HR-related programs. Futhermore, the survey results were used in the development of the market track study as well as the brand performance survey – the ambition being to synchronize those studies – and discussions were also initiated to integrate other third-party data such as blogs into the model. So one could say that what this ICT company was trying to do was to build a more jamming organization, and that they're following their progress through the surveys.

The five main capabilities that comprise the company's Future Capital Index are Insight, Change, Innovation, Talent and Sales. Each is based on one or more sub-indices that tap into crucial aspects of the strategy needed to handle

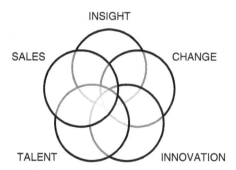

Figure 3.3   The five future-capabilities or T-habits

the challenges of the T-economy. Since these capabilities are at the core of what makes people dance, the following five chapters are dedicated to these principles and how to implement them in your organization. The principles will be outlined one by one in more detail, supported by research findings and examples. Most of the material and data has already been presented in various speeches, within client projects and so on, but are here combined into a bigger picture for the first time. Each chapter contains questions and recommendations as well as tables and graphs to make it easier to digest the general principles. In the end, one final chapter brings the picture together, giving hands-on tips on how to put the principles into action.

ARE YOU FIT FOR THE FUTURE?

Now, invest a few minutes in self-assessment. How big are your challenges, how prepared are you and your rivals to manage them, and what are the potential payoffs? Try to rate each of the aspects below on a scale from one to seven, where 1 = marginal challenge/not prepared at all/low payoff and 7 = massive challenge/world class preparedness/immense payoff.

	LEVEL OF CHALLENGE	OWN PREPAREDNESS	RIVAL PREPAREDNESS	POTENTIAL PAYOFF
Applying speed and long-term perspective simultaneously	1 2 3 4 5 6 7	1 2 3 4 5 6 7	1 2 3 4 5 6 7	1 2 3 4 5 6 7
Using analytics on external data	1 2 3 4 5 6 7	1 2 3 4 5 6 7	1 2 3 4 5 6 7	1 2 3 4 5 6 7
Having a visual and pattern-oriented approach to analytics	1 2 3 4 5 6 7	1 2 3 4 5 6 7	1 2 3 4 5 6 7	1 2 3 4 5 6 7
Applying metrics (KPI) on internal processes rather than outcomes	1 2 3 4 5 6 7	1 2 3 4 5 6 7	1 2 3 4 5 6 7	1 2 3 4 5 6 7
Building a thought culture: increasing thought productivity in individual and team work	1 2 3 4 5 6 7	1 2 3 4 5 6 7	1 2 3 4 5 6 7	1 2 3 4 5 6 7
Focusing on developing economies as markets	1 2 3 4 5 6 7	1 2 3 4 5 6 7	1 2 3 4 5 6 7	1 2 3 4 5 6 7
Seeing green technology as a business opportunity	1 2 3 4 5 6 7	1 2 3 4 5 6 7	1 2 3 4 5 6 7	1 2 3 4 5 6 7

(continued)

69

Continued

	LEVEL OF CHALLENGE	OWN PREPAREDNESS	RIVAL PREPAREDNESS	POTENTIAL PAYOFF
Competing from below: new high-quality low-cost competition	1 2 3 4 5 6 7	1 2 3 4 5 6 7	1 2 3 4 5 6 7	1 2 3 4 5 6 7
Leveraging on existing technologies rather than investing in new ones	1 2 3 4 5 6 7	1 2 3 4 5 6 7	1 2 3 4 5 6 7	1 2 3 4 5 6 7
Applying open innovation and systematic external innovation sourcing	1 2 3 4 5 6 7	1 2 3 4 5 6 7	1 2 3 4 5 6 7	1 2 3 4 5 6 7
Engaging all employees in innovation and ideas generation	1 2 3 4 5 6 7	1 2 3 4 5 6 7	1 2 3 4 5 6 7	1 2 3 4 5 6 7
Involving customers (and consumers) in innovation	1 2 3 4 5 6 7	1 2 3 4 5 6 7	1 2 3 4 5 6 7	1 2 3 4 5 6 7
Communicating through social media	1 2 3 4 5 6 7	1 2 3 4 5 6 7	1 2 3 4 5 6 7	1 2 3 4 5 6 7
Focusing on business concept innovation, rather than only incremental product development	1 2 3 4 5 6 7	1 2 3 4 5 6 7	1 2 3 4 5 6 7	1 2 3 4 5 6 7

Applying innovation as an interactive, experimental, evolutionary process	1 2 3 4 5 6 7	1 2 3 4 5 6 7	1 2 3 4 5 6 7	1 2 3 4 5 6 7
Creating challenging and goal-oriented team work	1 2 3 4 5 6 7	1 2 3 4 5 6 7	1 2 3 4 5 6 7	1 2 3 4 5 6 7
Delivering experiences and transformation to customers	1 2 3 4 5 6 7	1 2 3 4 5 6 7	1 2 3 4 5 6 7	1 2 3 4 5 6 7
Monitoring and managing brand appearance in social media	1 2 3 4 5 6 7	1 2 3 4 5 6 7	1 2 3 4 5 6 7	1 2 3 4 5 6 7
Managing employees as risk factors, not just as the core asset of the firm	1 2 3 4 5 6 7	1 2 3 4 5 6 7	1 2 3 4 5 6 7	1 2 3 4 5 6 7
Building a customer-centric rather than a company-centric business	1 2 3 4 5 6 7	1 2 3 4 5 6 7	1 2 3 4 5 6 7	1 2 3 4 5 6 7
Creating a future-oriented organization	1 2 3 4 5 6 7	1 2 3 4 5 6 7	1 2 3 4 5 6 7	1 2 3 4 5 6 7

To give the best possible effect, self-assessment should be a regularly reoccurring part of your routine, so use an erasable pen or take a copy of these pages before filling out the table.

Interpretation of self-assessment

Once you have filled out the table, the areas that you should focus on are those where the potential payoff is greater than the level of challenge and/or where your own organizational preparedness is lower than that of your rivals. Keep these areas in mind while reading the rest of the book, and feel free to revise your scores after finishing each chapter.

4

JAZZING UP THE DATA

> The quest for knowledge used to begin with grand theories. Now it begins with massive amounts of data. Welcome to the Petabyte Age.
>
> Chris Anderson, editor-in-chief of *Wired*[1]

In June 2008, *Wired*'s Chris Anderson proclaimed the end of science-as-we-know-it, welcoming us with the above words to the Petabyte Age. The reasons why the Petabyte Age is different are plenty. For once, we don't even have a working analogy for where we store today's huge amounts of information (not in folders, cabinets or libraries ... so in what?). But the fundamental reason is that we need to approach it differently, and that new approach will change our view of science. There's an increasing amount of data being collected for a reason, and that data is changing the name of the game.

We don't need models anymore, Anderson states. We have data. So will he be proven right? Are we seeing the end of science, at least in the form we've known it for the past 300 years or so? On one hand, there's a lot of evidence that Anderson might be right. The scientific approach, starting with hypotheses, building a model and testing it in order to understand the *why* is being replaced by analytics, searching for patterns. Correlation supersedes causality, and there are already several fields in which the new or non-scientific paradigm reigns. Finance is one where physicists and mathematicians took over decades ago, starting with empirical data instead of theories. Today, their data-driven stock trading accounts for half of the trading in the major stock markets, while traditional players are closing their trading departments.[2] In this world of big data reality supersedes the model – and financial markets are indeed a big-numbers game. So even though we might still need models in order to remember and create mental maps, we don't need them to win the game in the marketplace anymore. In that battle, correlations are enough.

On the other hand, one could say that what we're seeing isn't the end of science but instead the beginning of it. We no longer have to guess what's right and wrong, what's better or worse. We use data and analytics to discover, which in turn inspires us to build new models and theories. Not even during the heydays of scientific management and race biology were we so obsessed with science as we are today, so from this point of view we could easily claim that there's never been more science, and that society and business have never before been more scientific than they are today. Or, maybe, the end of science is just the end of the beginning of science. Then it's just the start that differs – philosophy and theory, or data and empiricism.

THE VALUE OF DATA

Facebook was founded by Mark Zuckerberg in 2004 as a college project. Since becoming more public, it has become a tremendous global success with 800 million active users.[3] But revenues have been slow up until recently, and Facebook has struggled to find a viable business model.[4]

Nevertheless, in May 2009 Russian Digital Sky acquired 1.96 percent of the company for USD 200 million, which equates to a total value of Facebook of over USD 10 billion.[5] Was Facebook really worth that much? Or more so, was worth its USD 66.5 billion implied valuation from September 2011[6] or USD 100 billion expected in November 2011[7]? Well, it depends. Considering the fact that Facebook's confirmed revenues from advertising have been low and that the company is yet to report officially any significant profit, the answer would be no. But in the light of what we've been discussing so far, and with a rumor spreading about Facebook doubling its half-year revenue to USD 1.6 billion in the first half of 2011, the company's value might well be close to USD 80 billion.[8] The future will show.

After the Digital Sky deal, Rob Salkowitz of Internet Evolution concluded that 'the overwhelming value of social networks is that they are gathering huge amounts of information about our interactions with one another, our relationships to content and media, our habits of using networks and data, and our interests. When mined correctly, these will yield market insights that will dramatically change the way businesses interact with their customers.'[9] Similarly, James Surowiecki, author of the blockbuster *The Wisdom of Crowds*,[10] said in a TED-talk in 2005 that 'what the blogosphere offers is the possibility of getting at the collective, distributed intelligence that is out there and we know is available to us if we can just figure out a way of accessing it'.[11] Today we more or less know how to do that.

MEASURING PERFORMANCE DRIVERS

Most larger companies spend a lot of time, energy and financial resources on finding out whether their employees are satisfied or not. They collect data about satisfaction, about their employees' views of the managers, whether the employees feel respected and whether they get to have a say. Most also ask their customers about how they perceive the services, and whether they are satisfied with product and service quality, with innovativeness and with the personal touch. On top of that, every company holds performance data, often available at the unit level, that describes financial and other performance indicators in detail.

But what do they do with that data? Do they link different data sets? Do they try to understand how important job satisfaction is to customer satisfaction and general performance, if satisfaction is the prime driver? Do they specifically analyze which individual and organizational practices contribute the most to organizational performance, innovation, or customer or employee satisfaction? Do they use the data to see whether the company has improved its *future capabilities*, if it's more fit for the future than the year before? In general the answer to most of those questions is no, and the reason for this is simple. Very few companies have yet applied the art of data-driven insight. Very few have yet realized that they live in the Petabyte Age and that there are vast quantities of data – and not only customer transaction data – that could be mined and used in the constant improvement game that is life. Data that could be used as a springboard into the future.

Let's, for example, take operational efficiency. In the Old World, *operational efficiency* had to do with the absence of internal and external friction, transaction costs, risk and other obstacles that made economic operations tiresome and costly. Today, however, its meaning has changed. When talking about operational efficiency today we mean simplicity, and by simplicity we mean speed, clarity, closeness, predictability and flexibility. I know this because I've taken in the need for data-driven insight and analyzed tens of thousands of employee responses from all parts of the world – responses to hundreds of questions related to organizational characteristics and practices.

If you try this (and you should), you'll find the patterns and see how different responses are related to each other. You'll find the *concept* of operational efficiency and how it's built from several interlinked components. And if you link those components to different performance indicators, such as managers' perception of their organization's performance compared to competitors, or to the customers' opinions of the organization, you'll see how different behaviors and characteristics drive performance. Table 4.1 is an example of such a result from one of our client projects. It shows a ranking of aspects of operational efficiency that are closely linked to organizational performance. The ranking might be slightly different in your organization, but it will probably not look that different since most such patterns are fairly universal.

Over the years Kairos Future has applied this kind of research to identify the key performance drivers in the New World, in the T-economy. We have studied aspects of

Table 4.1   Aspects of operational efficiency

OPERATIONAL EFFICIENCY DRIVERS
Simple work processes
Speedy decision-making
Rapid implementation
Policy flexibility
Access to information and people
Clear organization

strategy, sales, leadership, innovation, business intelligence and change management in a number of large-scale projects and how practices in those fields correlate to or predict different aspects of performance. What we have been interested in are the practices, behaviors, and cultural and practical aspects that might provide guidance not only on what to do, but also on *how* to do it. As I wrote in Chapter 3, a few years ago we were presented with the opportunity combine the research into a full-scale global project for one of the largest ICT companies in the world. In the following chapters I will present some of the conclusions from that project as well as from a number of supporting and parallel research projects.

INSIGHT EXCELLENCE

After years of having data-driven insight as a foundation for our consulting business, we have found seven key performance drivers. The rest of this chapter is dedicated to these cornerstones.

Structured processes

As we saw in Chapter 2, systematic planning and procedures is one of the three linchpins of a jamming organization. In insight and foresight, the process is key to getting a result, and it is critical to productivity. In order for creativity to flourish and for new ways of thinking to be adapted into the organization, a robust and somewhat conservative foundation is needed. Without structured processes forming a firm ground, new ideas will simply not have a stable enough platform from which to lever themselves. Establishing processes for frequent analysis but at the same

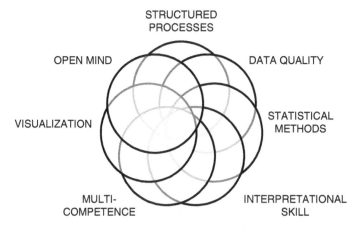

STRUCTURED
PROCESSES

OPEN MIND

DATA QUALITY

VISUALIZATION

STATISTICAL
METHODS

MULTI-
COMPETENCE

INTERPRETATIONAL
SKILL

Figure 4.1 The cornerstones of insight excellence

time being open for new ways of thinking and working is therefore a matter of balance – a balance to which we will return.

Data quality

'Garbage in, garbage out' is an old and still valid saying. True insight is always based on high-quality data. But remember, the requirements on the data quality also depend on the purpose. If you need precise figures about what people think about web-based interaction between patients and doctors you probably shouldn't base that analysis on a web-based questionnaire, but rather on face-to-face interviews with a representative random sample. On the other hand, if you're interested in how health or healthcare is discussed, what the key topics are, how they differ between countries and so forth, a web-panel is probably OK, especially if you're keen on the views of younger respondents. It might even be relevant to skip traditional data collection and start mining discussion groups and blogs right away. Or if you're interested in the discussions in the traditional media you could do the same with online newspapers. In online media you'll find large amounts of information that can be structured and analyzed to provide you with a conceptual understanding of what health is.

That's exactly what we did in an international project a couple of years ago for one of the leading multinationals in the food and beverage industry. In order to understand the health field in a set of European countries we followed the discussions in blogs and discussion groups and conceptually mapped the discussions using our own tools for automated text analysis. This gave us valuable insights, but we complemented the analysis with ethnographic in-depth interviews that gave us a deeper understanding of some of the issues. Finally, to get the numbers right, we carried out a survey to quantify the opinions and patterns identified through the blogs and discussion groups. The results gave the client a whole new understanding of the brand in its focus and context, identified a number of unexploited opportunities and set a new direction for product development and communication.

Figure 4.2 shows a conceptual map developed in another project. It shows the top six aspects of luxury as expressed in the Chinese blogosphere. Using different methods/ analyses, the concepts can be plotted on a two-dimensional map where the analyst interprets the axes. In this case, we can see that the Chinese connect luxury primarily with such material things as cars, goods and buildings and luxury activities like cruising and hotels. I can tell you that the luxury map looks completely different in a Swedish or

US context. For Swedes, for instance, luxury is primarily associated with *Cozy Friday*,[12] lit candles and a nice dinner at home. It is about everyday experiences.

Blogs, micro blogs, discussion groups, online news and so forth are just a few sources of information that can be continuously gathered, sorted and analyzed. Together with internally generated business and market data they are one of the most valuable assets that a firm can ever compile. With the rapidly growing amount of data it's easy to understand that data-driven strategies are perceived as the strongest trend in the consulting world today.[13] But beware: what counts first and foremost is the quality (and control) – not the quantity – of data. For instance, business data changes at an average rate of four percent a month,[14] so you have to make sure that the data you're analyzing is still relevant.

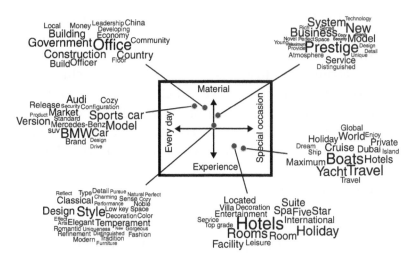

Figure 4.2 Example of output from an analysis of Chinese blog posts about luxury

Statistical methods

Analytics is the intelligent treatment of complex data with the use of statistical methods. I really want to stress this, so let's make it exceedingly clear:

- Spreadsheets are not analytics
- All spreadsheet users are not analysts

OK? Good. Statistical methods could be applied on almost any data set, whether open or in-house. Above, I illustrate what can be done with one type of data, namely blog posts. Below is another example – in this case using all Chinese invention patents registered since 1985, which amounts to well over two million patents. In order to organize this patent registration data we have used geographical data as well as patent classification and identified the 50 largest geographical patent clusters in China today. This analysis provides a series of conclusions never before reported, the main contribution being three distinct waves of the Chinese invention landscape, of which the third wave is the entrepreneurial wave.[15] Figure 4.3 illustrates the growth of the clusters in terms of patents in just one year (between 2009 and 2010). The axes indicate the number of patenting entities (X) and the patent growth rate (Y) respectively, while the size of the circles corresponds to the number of patents in the cluster.

Interpretational skill

The rapidly changing nature of our times means that the individual paying for the information doesn't have time to digest the actual intelligence that's being served. Instead, the data has to be interpreted and understood before it be

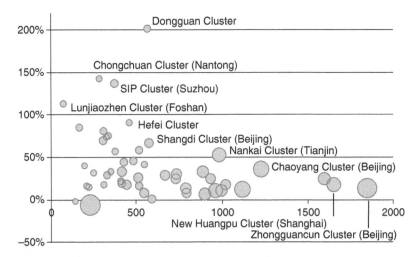

Figure 4.3 The 50 patent clusters with the highest annual registration of patents in mainland China

brought to a client or employer. What they want is the synopsis, the quick summary – and preferably abridged into a single PowerPoint slide (or, even better, into something like Gapminder or Pivot). In the New World, being a master of turning your interpretations into visual illustration and graphs is normally the way to *Aha!*, so just bringing forward the data isn't usually enough. The interpretation of the axis in the illustration of the Chinese luxury blogs is a simple, but yet powerful adaptation of that.

But even though data and fancy graphics are increasingly important, when push comes to shove they're merely data and graphics. What creates real value is the interpretation and the conclusions that you make, and the *naming and framing* that you connect to those conclusions. The ability to create concepts and expressions that summarize, communicate and place things in a context is one of the most coveted talents in the Public Relations industry. Just

83

think of trends and concepts like *the cloud* or *High Tech/ High Touch* (by John Naisbitt)[16] – where the expressions themselves have become etched into the minds of many, making us remember a whole lot about the concepts – and you'll see what I mean.

Multi-competence

The strength of your analytics team is its variety. By employing analysts with multiple competences – data crunching and the ability to interpret, present and communicate results – as well as analysts with different backgrounds, perspectives and experiences will make it easier to detect the subtleties that young trends usually are. The plurality of the analytics team also facilitates internal collaboration as the relations between different departments are less likely to be strained when they aren't occupied by a certain *type of people*.

Visualization

Using all available data in a creative way is one of the future-maker's areas of expertise. The key word here is *creative*. As people become less and less enthusiastic about processing large amounts of written information, new means of communication have to be invented. We've already looked at the new presentation techniques Gapminder and Pivot, which are of course revolutionary in their field. But excellent visualization can come in many other shapes too, and sometimes it's even as simple as finding a clever way of presenting lots of information in a single picture. One such example that Kairos Future has used in a recent blog analysis is a calendar illustrating the frequency of experiences-related key words occurring in Swedish blogs over the year.[17] While the same information in text would have been tedious both to write and read, the calendar gives a schematic overview that can be taken in very quickly. So putting some effort into visualization clearly helps communication.

At the other end, visualizing information can of course also be rather complex. The latest services come in the shape of augmented or amplified reality, which is based on a visual data layer that's placed on top of what you can see with your own eyes. Since 2010, Google Goggles has allowed provided users with information about landmarks, wine and books just from them taking pictures of them on their iPhones; pictures of labels, logos or barcodes bring up information on where to purchase the product and what it will cost. It is also possible to photograph text that you want translated or business cards that you want entered into your contacts.[18] The Nordic eyeglasses chain Synsam allows its customers to try out glasses from Cheap Monday using augmented reality and a webcam,[19] Facebook has launched facial recognition in order to increase name-tagging of pictures submitted by its users,[20] and both Ford and General Motors have used augmented reality in different marketing campaigns. Many other applications are sure to come.

Open mind

We have already seen plenty of examples of what the new scientific approach might bring about: start with the totality and nail it down to the details. Use mathematics, explore and see what you get rather than start with a theory and search for evidence. That's what experiments and sites such as We Feel Fine, PatientsLikeMe, Mappiness and OkCupid all do. That's what Husqvarna did when they searched for the passions of true gardeners, and that's what the European Travel Commission did when it studied the Chinese image of some European countries in a study performed by Kairos Future in 2011. And, most of all, it's what Google does all the time.

Google didn't have the best theory about culture and online advertising. In fact, they had no theory at all. But they had the data and the best analytical tools and they were convinced that with that in place, they would win one day. This fundamentally different view of the world – that we don't need to know *why* things work; it's enough to know *that* it works – actually seems to be the founding philosophy of Google. They simply accept that they don't know why one webpage is better than another. If statistics say it is, that's good

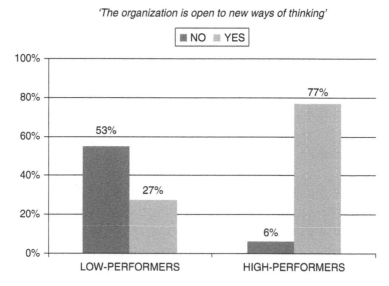

'The organization is open to new ways of thinking'

Figure 4.4 The relation between overall performance and an open mind

enough. And that's also the reason why Google can translate languages or match ads with searches. It's simply statistics.

Naturally, having such an open mind is critical to success in all kinds of intellectual activities, including insight work. Figure 4.4 shows just how important it is. In short, it shows that openness is 3 times more common among high-performing companies than among low-performers. So get ready to challenge your preconceptions and let the data lead the way. Don't ignore *uncomfortable* results or results that challenge what you thought you knew, because only when data guides action is your organization truly analytics-driven!

DANCING WITH THE DATA

Self-assessment is the first step towards succeeding in the T-economy. Are you prepared to get quantitative in the Petabyte age?

CORNERSTONE	MEANING	ARE YOU FIT FOR THE FUTURE?	ASSESSMENT
STRUCTURED PROCESSES	Developing processes for frequent analysis	Is systematic planning and thought-out procedure the foundation of your analytical processes?	☐ YES ☐ NO
DATA QUALITY	Using data that's relevant and up-to-date is more important than the quantity of it	Do you consciously choose what data to use and when?	☐ YES ☐ NO
STATISTICAL METHODS	Intelligent treatment of complex data with the use of statistical methods	Does your team have sufficient statistical knowledge and proficiency, and are they given enough time to use it?	☐ YES ☐ NO
INTERPRETATIONAL SKILL	What creates real value is the interpretation and conclusions that you make	Is your team capable both of high-quality analysis and of summarizing the results in a communicative, efficient and creative format?	☐ YES ☐ NO

MULTI-COMPETENCE	Employing analysts with diverse competences	Does your team encompass a mixture of competencies and personal traits?	☐ YES ☐ NO
VISUALIZATION	Being a master of visual illustration and graphs	Are you constantly searching for new ways of presenting things and new ways of generating *Aha!* experiences?	☐ YES ☐ NO
OPEN MIND	Letting data lead the way despite any uncomfortable, counterintuitive results	Do you trust your analytical tools enough to let them guide your actions, that is, to be truly analytics-driven?	☐ YES ☐ NO

5

WALTZING INTO THE FUTURE

It is good to have an end to journey towards,
but it is the journey that matters in the end.
Ursula K. Le Guin, US author[1]

During the 1990s the business landscape in most industries became more turbulent due to globalization and rapid technological change. This shift gave birth to a new stream of both popular and academic management research dealing with strategy and management under uncertainty, a condition that most businesses today face. Strategy scholars and researchers turned from a static view of strategy to a more dynamic one, emphasizing general and dynamic abilities (flexibility, adaptivity, strategy innovation and so on). Thus, focus shifted from *finding and defending a position* to *adapting and constantly reinventing the company*. A more dynamic world requires the ability to place layers of competence upon older layers. Dancing with the future is therefore at the core of what a future strategist does.

The concept of dynamic abilities was originally outlined in 1997 by Teece, Pisano and Shuen as 'an answer to the Schumpeterian world of innovation based competition, price/performance rivalry, increasing returns, and the creative destruction of existing competences'.[2] Since then, numerous academics and management writers have leaned on the concept: in later years researchers such as Hamel and Valinkangas,[3] Kim and Mauborgne,[4] and Rumelt.[5] What all these scholars emphasize is the combination of the ability to foresee what's coming, to conceptualize a response and to act proactively.

However, the ability to do so isn't simply a set of managerial practices – what companies do. More than this, it's part of what companies *are*. It's embedded in the corporate DNA, a matter of culture. However, this doesn't mean that it's impossible to acquire the desired dynamic abilities of foresight or contextual orientation, proactivity or change. By identifying and communicating the desired cultural elements, and by implementing supporting practices and behaviors, it is possible to change.

GETTING TO THE FUTURE FIRST

The only way to win the battle of the future is to get to the future first; but if you manage to do it, being a master of future-making has its benefits. Surprisingly enough, many organizations are still battling with day-to-day problem-solving and firefighting. Why? Because of shortsightedness and neglected strategic work. Such carelessness exposes the business to unnecessary risk as the causes of daily catastrophes are never identified. Naturally, an organization that can't handle today will not have a proactive approach to the future either.

What you need to do is to get a serious grip of your future by putting it into action now. Having the future as a starting point for your thinking and acting will eventually put you a few steps ahead of the game, which means no fires to put out. Figure 5.1 comes from one of our own studies and illustrates the path to success that awaits those who identify new opportunities, launch innovative new products

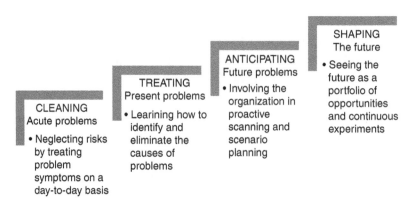

Figure 5.1   The path towards shaping the future

and services, and design an organization for the future. The more diverse one's strategic repertoire and the more distant the time horizons taken into account when selecting from this tactical arsenal, the more proactive and hence successful an organization can be when facing the future.

Being the one who knows the industry and where it's heading makes it possible not only to prepare for the future, but to make actions towards changing it too. This is why automobile companies present concept cars at fairs. Even though these fantasy machines are rarely introduced to the market they are a way for the brands to boast of their knowledge about what's coming next. The prophecies cast by the leading brands tend to be self-fulfilling too as the expo cars set new goals for the industry that rivaling producers start chasing.

CHANGE EXCELLENCE

When you're dancing with the future like a world champion while others stumble around stepping on each other's toes, people will notice. In the business context, being noticed makes it easier to attract customers as well as talented employees as they're drawn towards the thought leader in your industry. Showing off your intellectual head start makes you interesting as an employer, partner and supplier, which will give valuable input to the next new thing. But what is needed in order to climb from fire extinguishing towards shaping the future? What are the habits that today separate the winners from the losers? Figure 5.2 illustrates (in clockwise order of importance) the seven most critical success factors in this game – factors that I first identified in my doctoral dissertation[6] ten years ago and which have later been identified in several more recent research projects.

What I found to be the most important success factor is competitive scanning: keeping track of rivals' and clients movements in the market. In fact, the first, third, fourth and sixth points all cover organizational behaviors and activities related to business environment analysis and strategic conversation about the changing landscape, its opportunities and possible strategic moves. Consequently,

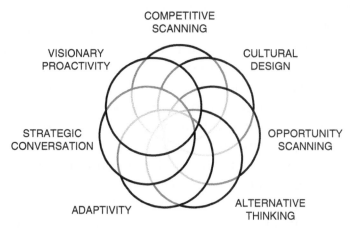

Figure 5.2 The cornerstones of change excellence

activities linked to trend analysis and contextual analysis are undoubtedly critical to an organization's long-term success, as is visionary proactivity: the ambition to *change the name of the game* or *shape the future*.

Furthermore, other research has shown that the organizations that make the most of business environment analysis (that is, trend analysis, consumer insight, competitive analysis and so on) are those that have a clear organization for the analysis and in which this work is considered a top priority by top management.[7] Such an organization involves a systematic and continuous approach, a clear strategy for integration of the results into the business planning, innovation and other types of decision-making, a clear and easy communication of results to key stakeholders and recipients, a shared language and a clear information structure. The rest of this chapter deals with these issues.

Competitive scanning

Do you know what your rivals and clients are thinking and doing right now? And how much do you think they know about your current strategies and plans? Being able to predict your competitor's actions at the same time as you throw surprises at them is an important skill in all fast moving markets, and it is created by knowledge. Equally important is to have an in-depth understanding of where your clients and prospects are moving in order to come up with winning proposals. You need to be close to both your clients and your rivals. If you're not continuously gathering, sorting and analyzing large amounts of data and other business intelligence information, the chances are that your rivals are already ahead of you. This is most certainly true in mature and highly competitive industries. As we learned in Chapter 4, a data-driven strategy is key not only to the ability to follow the moves of competitors and clients in the market, but also to fast action on new intelligence.

Cultural design

OK, but how about culture? Do we really need to implement processes for capturing opportunities and challenges in the business landscape? Couldn't an ongoing dialogue about the challenges and opportunities – in the management team as well as during coffee breaks – be just as powerful? The answer is no. Having an outward and forward-looking culture is good, even necessary, but it can never replace implemented procedures. Tailoring a culture that supports the intended strategy and implementing the future in the organization is therefore crucial.

In fact, cultural design or *being the dream* seems to be one of the factors in organizational success. When people feel that the overall vision and direction is implemented in the organization's culture and ways of working, there's an alignment between intention and action, between brand promises and brand experience. If we are what we intend to be, we do what we intend to do. And research that we have performed for a global ICT company shows that cultural design isn't only strongly correlated with perceived organizational performance. It is also one of the strongest drivers of customer satisfaction. So do as you say, make future now, be a good role model and implement the culture that you want to have.

Opportunity scanning

Like competitive scanning, opportunity scanning requires a methodical procedure to identify trends and opportunities in the market. Actually, the two are very closely related: spotting rival and customer actions inside and – perhaps even more importantly – outside your industry will often reveal new possible directions of business development.

Figure 5.3 has its origin in one of our global studies, in which managers in nine countries evaluated the competencies of their organizations. It illustrates the importance of a systematic approach in the opportunity-scanning context, displayed as proportions of high-performers in two groups of organizations. In companies where managers say that there's no systematic process for identifying opportunities, less than 33 percent say that their performance is higher than their competitors' – compared with almost 77 percent in companies where managers say that they do have such a process in place. Furthermore, studies of the impact of systematic scanning on customer satisfaction show even stronger relations. So clearly 'systematic' matters!

Alternative thinking

Humans are scenario-planning creatures by nature, and this skill is the main reason why we're still around. That may also be true for Shell – the corporate champion of scenario planning. Had they not been meticulously planning for alternate futures since the 1970s they might not have survived the multitude of blows against their brand – blows from bad publicity on everything from environmental issues and safety measures to human rights violations – that have haunted them over the past decades.[8]

Although we don't always appreciate them, alternatives are good. Organizations who are capable of divergent thinking, scenario planning and forming competing

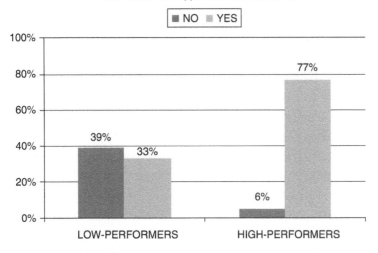

Figure 5.3 The relation between overall performance and systematic opportunity scanning

strategies or ideas do not only tend to be more successful than others. Interestingly, alternative thinking also seems to be appreciated by customers. An analysis of the links between organizational habits and practices and different aspects of customer performance shows that organizations that systematically evaluate different alternatives when solving non-routine problems are much better at supporting customers in innovation activities. In fact, divergent thinking seems to be one of the strongest performance drivers according to customers.

Adaptivity

One of the central components in the challenge facing managers and organizations is the speed and quality of actions required to stay in pace with one's competitors. Lewis Carroll's story of Alice and the Queen in *Through the Looking-Glass* illustrates the nature of fast-moving worlds. Alice notices that she doesn't move, although she's running fast, and when she notices that, the queen says that she must be from a very slow world. In a fast-moving world you have to run for your life just to stay where you are, and run twice as fast in order to get anywhere, she explains.[9]

Whether we like it or not, to most companies the world is running at an ever faster speed. Time and progress march on, so to speak, but at a Moore's law's pace instead of a clock's. Figure 5.4 illustrates the importance of time horizons, comparing the requirements of the Old World to that of the new one. While the Old World allowed and even rewarded thinking before acting and *waiting-to-seeing*, the opposite is true nowadays. Traditional planning has played out its role, since well-researched and detailed plans are often dated before the ink has dried. What matters today instead is speedy action. But rapid decision-making and action aren't enough either. Running at the speed of light is no use if you run in the wrong direction. Therefore speedy action needs to be combined with long-view thinking. Management is more like driving a car at high speed: in order to survive you need to keep your eyes focused far up the road. You need to be able to be both flexible *and* foresighted.

What Figure 5.4 shows is that the saying '*if you snooze you lose*' doesn't only have to do with alarm clocks, but with slow market actions as well. If you've missed the first bus, there's no use in making a run for the second one: you'll just reach the destination last and out of breath. In that case, the best strategy instead is to wait until more information is available. If you're lucky, the ones that didn't snooze and therefore caught the first bus will by then have

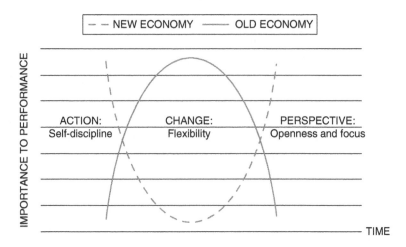

Figure 5.4 The relative importance of different time horizons now and then

discovered that the bus in fact went in the wrong direction. Thus, a quick decision not to decide until later used to be a weakness in the Old World, but is now a potential performance booster.

Strategic conversation

Although plans will never take us to the future, planning might. And in planning the critical word seems to be *'systematic'*. In *How to Get Control of Your Time and Your Life*, time management guru Allen Lakein proposed a system in which every man should write down his or her priorities as long-term, medium-term and short-term life goals and then sort them into order of importance.[10] One of the people who followed his advice was former US president Bill Clinton, which he revealed in the preface in his autobiography *My Life*.[11]

Lakein's advice is as valid today as when he wrote it in the 1970s. However, planning in organizations is more complicated. It's not enough to take down the organization's priorities and sort them. They need to be part of an open and ongoing dialogue about changes in the business landscape and where to go. Plans and goals need to be communicated, and since achieving them involves many people's joint efforts there need to be supporting processes and procedures in place. By communicating the purpose of proposed changes clearly to the entire organization, the firm's preparedness rises dramatically – as does the possibility of getting good input to the process from all corners of the organization.

Visionary proactivity

Fast growing companies exist in every industry, in boom as well as in bust. But what is it that distinguishes fast growers from more ordinary companies? They have other reference points! Fast growers expect higher growth levels. For the fast grower, a growth rate of 10–20 percent or more is expected, while for others even 5–10 percent is considered very good. Visionary proactivity is about trying to be a future-maker that changes the game and exploits potential opportunities. In order to do that, big-picture thinking or *reaching for the stars* is fundamental.

Visions have occurred in different forms and under different names throughout history. For almost every social science, visions (in different terms) are seen as essential to humans as well as to organizations and societies. From modern sports psychology we're all aware of the consequences of *bad thinking*. What separates the winners from the ordinary isn't so much the physics as it is the mind. When golf player Annika Sörenstam set a new standard in women's golf in the late 1990s it was based on new thinking and new reference points. 'Why use four strikes on this par four hole when you could do it in three', she thought and set out for birdies.[12]

Strategy researchers Fiegenbaum, Hart and Schendel proposed that what's true for individuals also works on the organizational level. Their conclusions, based on literature research, are presented in Table 5.1 and show that, just like individuals, organizations need constantly moving reference points to cope with the changing business environment. Organizational behavior changes as organizations move beyond their reference points; or in other words, when they pass their goals or visions. Below the reference point the organization is *up and coming*, while above it it behaves as a defender of past success. Thus, it's necessary to think in visions, and to rethink the visions constantly.[13]

Table 5.1 Strategic choice behavior according to Fiegenbaum et al.

	ABOVE REFERENCE POINT	BELOW REFERENCE POINT
CURRENT SITUATION:	Satisfied	Dissatisfied
	Sitting on top of the world	At the bottom looking up
PERCEPTION OF NEW ISSUES:	Threat	Opportunity
	Potential loss	Potential gain
	Negative	Positive
ORGANIZATIONAL PROCESSES:	Constricted	Open
	Rigid	Flexible
	Centralized	Decentralized
NATURE OF RESPONSE OR BEHAVIOR:	Risk-averse	Risk-taking
	Conservative	Daring
	Defensive	Offensive

History is full of excellent vision-driven organizations and individuals that have gone beyond their own reference-points ... into mediocrity and failure! Without moving reference-points, you might become one of them, while if you make sure to keep the carrot at a challenging distance, you might in fact move beyond anticipations. To become a true future-maker or future-shaper, it's not enough to anticipate and react to what others do. You need to be the one that takes the lead, the one that makes the new moves, that reinvents the industry. And since the future isn't given, this needs to be an act of experimental searching.

DANCING WITH THE FUTURE

Self-assessment is the first step towards succeeding in the T-economy. Are you prepared to change the future before it changes you?

CORNERSTONE	MEANING	ARE YOU FIT FOR THE FUTURE?	ASSESSMENT
COMPETITIVE SCANNING	Employing a systematic process to follow the moves of competitors	Do you know what your rivals are doing and planning right now?	☐ YES ☐ NO
CULTURAL DESIGN	Tailoring a culture that supports the intended strategy	Is the strategic direction of your company reflected in the way you carry out your work?	☐ YES ☐ NO
OPPORTUNITY SCANNING	Methodically identifying trends and opportunities in the market	Is there a systematic process in place for identifying new trends and opportunities in the market, and are people in your company in general curious about the future?	☐ YES ☐ NO
ALTERNATIVE THINKING	Applying divergent thinking and scenario planning to strategies	Do you systematically employ methods such as a trend-mapping or scenario planning to analyze possible future developments?	☐ YES ☐ NO

(continued)

103

Continued

CORNERSTONE	MEANING	ARE YOU FIT FOR THE FUTURE?	ASSESSMENT
ADAPTIVITY	Adapting to changing circumstances without concern for past practices	Is your company open to changes in ways of working, or are habitual routines hard to change?	☐ YES ☐ NO
STRATEGIC CONVERSATION	Having an open dialogue about changes in the business landscape and where to go	Does everyone in your company know and understand the strategic direction of the company, and does everyone actively contribute to it?	☐ YES ☐ NO
VISIONARY PROACTIVITY	Reaching for the stars and constantly exceeding anticipations	Is your company more opportunity-maximizing than risk-minimizing?	☐ YES ☐ NO

6

GETTING INTO THE SWING OF THINGS

I haven't failed. I've found 10,000 ways that
don't work.
Thomas Alva Edison, US inventor, scientist
and businessman (1847–1931)[1]

Since the mid-1990s, innovation has become the number
one buzzword in academia as well as in business. The reason
is simple. In a world with a growing customer deficit and
hypercompetition the ability to deliver new services and
products – and even to reinvent the company itself – has
become crucial for long-term survival. It seems self-evident,
but has also been shown to be right by rigid academic research.
In the software industry, for example, the annual failure rate
has been found to be several times higher for companies with
a low innovation rate, compared to those with a high innovation rate.[2] Similarly, in 2010, the international management
consulting firm Arthur D. Little published a report about
innovation excellence, showing that top innovators not only
expand their existing businesses, but are also much more active
in new business and new product development. Arthur D.
Little also found 'that the most innovative global companies
achieve up to twice as many sales, as much as double the EBIT
and take half the time to break even when they introduce new
products and services, compared to the average company'.[3]

It should be no surprise that innovative companies specialize in innovation. We've already discussed the need for concept and business innovation (like the iPod and iPhone, which were much more than products); open innovation approaches (such as Procter & Gamble's *Connect+Develop*), which Arthur D. Little found to be more common among top innovators; and the need for many innovations instead of just a few. Nevertheless, since we know that innovation is highly correlated with survival, sales and profitability the question isn't whether innovation is a good strategic priority. Instead, the question is how your company can become one of these innovators.

PLAYFUL THINKING, SERIOUS PLAYING AND GENEROUS GARDENING

Using a metaphor, innovative companies are like kids: they search, they play and they have nurturing parents supporting their activities. The reason is simple: kids are in the business of quick learning. Each day is full of newness and needs to be understood and conquered. The same goes for companies facing a challenging and – due to others' innovations – rapidly changing world. Thus, we can identify three core characteristics of innovative companies. (You recognize them from Chapter 2, don't you?)

- **Playful thinkers**. Innovative companies are eager to understand the customers and the business landscape they're navigating. They're open to new ways of thinking and eager to involve others and synthesize what they experience.

- **Serious players**. Innovative companies don't just think. They constantly try out new solutions, new models and new proposals, and they apply low-cost experimentation to everything they do, and they play together with others.

■ **Generous gardeners**. Innovative companies nurture an open, sharing and generous culture that supports playfulness and searching. They have people personally committed to innovation, and a well-functioning infrastructure that supports smooth and rapid innovation.

INNOVATION EXCELLENCE

The extensive global research that we've performed for one of the leading ICT companies confirms that successful innovation combines conceptual thinking, wild thinking and a systematic approach. Innovation unites radical change with incremental steps, new businesses with improved offerings, induced methodology with spontaneous creativity and business renewal with new ways of working. And behind it all is a balanced combination of inspiration and structured processes.

One of the sub-indices that we created in the ICT project was devised to measure a company's innovative capacity. The factors most strongly correlated with firm performance are listed in Figure 6.1, in clockwise order of importance starting at noon. In the rest of this chapter, we'll dig deeper into each one of these success factors.

Customer and user insights

Just a few decades ago, *innovation* was exclusively a R&D-heavy process originating in science labs and generating output in the form of patents. However, not even the technology industry still sees innovation as just technological

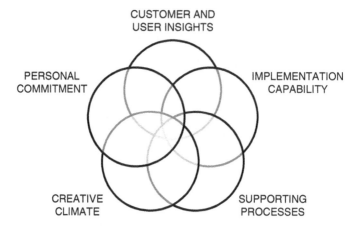

Figure 6.1 The cornerstones of innovation excellence

innovation. Today, the most important innovation proficiency is one in which trying new ideas, involving customers and turning these insights into concepts and actions constitutes the core of the innovation process. As the value of products and services shifts from the product and service itself to its experience-creating and transformative power, innovation becomes more of a matter of interaction with users, customers and consumers. Such interactive innovation – often referred to as co-creation or open source innovation – has consequently become much more common. This intimate relationship with customers, as well as its consequences, forms one of the major shifts of our time and has therefore been given a chapter of its own later on in the book (Chapter 8).

Implementation capability

Speed matters more and more – both in decision-making and in the implementation of business decisions. In a fast-moving world you never get a second chance. You need to be quick and correct, and if you aren't, you're in deep trouble. Smooth and rapid decision-making, access to information and decision-makers. and rapid implementation are all key success drivers. And for those accessible decision-makers, the secret lies in being good at adapting to changing circumstances without too much concern for past practice.

Figure 6.2 comes from one of our own research projects and illustrates the link between overall perceived performance among managers across the world and their perceived implementation speed. For those that rate their implementation speed as high more than two times as many (75 percent compared to 30 percent) also rate their performance as high compared to their competitors. Although the figure is based on self-responded data, results

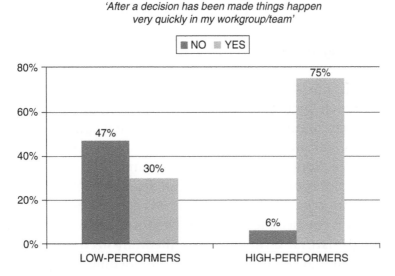

'After a decision has been made things happen very quickly in my workgroup/team'

Figure 6.2 The relation between overall performance and rapid implementation

are similar when we look at relations between for instance customer satisfaction and speed. The simple conclusion is: Speed is crucial. It's no longer enough to be right. You need to be right *now*!

The firm's implementation capability, like many other things, depends on how well-greased the organizational machinery is. This is especially true when it comes to innovation. Very few entrepreneurs are successful the first time because they're inexperienced and too unsystematic. Normally, most of their ideas don't get the attention they deserve while others get far too much attention – either because there are no alternatives or because the ideas came from a certain direction. Having well-defined and well-used processes to generate and capture ideas and them into valuable innovations matters more than the quality of each specific idea. In fact, innovation is more about transpiration than it is about inspiration, so you have to experiment, to try and try in order to succeed, just as Edison noted.

Supporting processes

All firms possess some kind of product development process, which in theory goes from idea to market success. But what about the ideas? Where do they come from? A creative culture is of course necessary, but never enough. If you're hopelessly stuck in the pursuit of The Great Innovation you will probably not relax if I tell you that the more competitive your business environment is, the greater is the need for *many* innovations. Surprising to me though, is that although most medium-sized and larger companies at least in theory have a documented process for taking new ideas to market, very few have a systematic process for generating and evaluating ideas aimed at creating more ideas at a higher quality. The challenge is therefore to create an *innovation machine* that systematically does that.

The *general-to-specific* approach to innovation – the innovation machine illustrated in Figure 6.3 – allows for true creativity and process focus at the same time as it reduces the cost of idea generation. Opening up for diverse thinking and input from all sources imaginable and then filtering these very strictly will improve both the amount and the quality of ideas that reach the first tollgate at which any money needs to be invested into the innovation itself. Since expenses tend to grow exponentially at each tollgate from idea to launch (represented by the size of the squares in the figure), a thorough scan of a multitude of ideas before they even reach initial investment is of course a practice that saves money.

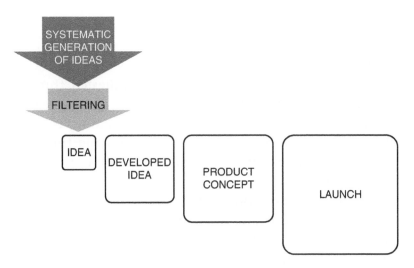

Figure 6.3   The innovation machine

Arthur D. Little's report, mentioned at the beginning of this chapter, shows that such innovation machines or *innovation engines* come in at least three different shapes. According to the report, the automotive and software industries prefer an analysis-driven innovation engine, heavy with strategies and planning based on product life cycles, while doing business in pharmaceuticals or oil requires a research-driven innovation engine, rich in scientifically generated ideas among which a winning portfolio is carefully selected over a long period of time. What is, however, suitable for most businesses – to those dealing in fast-moving consumer goods, services, telecom and chemicals to name a few – is the idea-driven innovation engine. This machine is fed with a large number of ideas collected and generated upstream – which are enhanced further down the funnel so that nearly all of them can be executed downstream. And if you're lucky, The Great Innovation might just follow.

Creative climate

At the very foundation of all other innovation abilities is the organization's overall creativity, manifested through each employee's attitude. An organization with a creative climate has an intrinsic drive for understanding customers and business landscapes and for improving thinking. This makes way for implementation based on knowledge rather than guesswork. Figure 6.4 adapts a concept from my doctoral dissertation[4] and illustrates how innovations are applied in successful firms. Organizations that learn to handle all three levels of the pyramid will find that the whole is greater than the sum of its parts, while others that fail to summon all the necessary building blocks will be

POSTURE
Boldness and speed

- Adaptive and not afraid of risks
- Speedly decisions and implementation
- Improvement plans are implemented

PROCESSES
From business context to new offering

- Good internal collaboration betweeen units
- Targets, roles and responsibilities are clear
- Improvements are followed up and implemented

CULTURE
Creative climate

- Good internal collaboration within units
- Personal authority is given, accountability is assumed
- A diverse and engaging workplace

Figure 6.4 Organizational practices driving performance

left wondering what went wrong. Relatively simple things such as team spirit and leadership are what give birth to and nurture a creative climate, without which a firm can never be innovative.

Personal commitment

The last piece of a firm's innovation puzzle is held by its employees. Having your staff personally committed to bringing in new ideas and supporting innovation is perhaps what gives the largest ripple effect into the rest of the business. But what creates committed employees? Well, the drivers of dedication vary slightly both between countries and industries. For instance, in egalitarian societies (such as the Scandinavian countries) clearly defined responsibilities and good pay are far less important drivers of enthusiasm than in more hierarchal and uncertainty-avoiding countries such as South Korea, Spain and France.[5] However, studies in the field normally point out three things: the ability to influence job conditions, a stimulating environment and supportive colleagues.[6]

The main reason why people lack commitment and feel alienated or frustrated is that they experience lack of authority and influence – and that often seems more true for younger people. In several international studies we have found that authority and influence explains almost half of the motivational gap between younger and older employees, so if the young in your organization are less committed than your older employees, remember that you're not alone. This lack of devotion is a global trend.

In comparison with satisfaction, commitment is more of a personality factor and as such is much harder to change. Still, most employees can become dedicated. Although commitment itself can't be *generated* by the direct actions of managers or leaders, it is affected by the engagement of other team members. Being part of an energizing team with an open climate, great cooperation and a knowledge-seeking and sharing approach seems to be the things that drive devotion. Commitment is contagious and – importantly – it comes from inside. But let's get back to all this in the next chapter.

DANCING WITH IDEAS

Self-assessment is the first step towards succeeding in the T-economy. Are you prepared to build an innovation machine?

CORNERSTONE	MEANING	ARE YOU FIT FOR THE FUTURE?	ASSESSMENT
CUSTOMER AND USER INSIGHTS	Trying out new concepts and involving customers in innovation	Does your company involve customers and users in all stages of the innovation process?	☐ YES ☐ NO
IMPLEMENTATION CAPABILITY	Having well-defined and used processes that turn ideas into valuable innovations	Do you have the means to help turn ideas from employees into business or improvement proposals and market insights into new products and offers?	☐ YES ☐ NO
SUPPORTING PROCESSES	Building a *machine* that carries the innovation process from idea to launch	Are you constantly scanning a multitude of ideas, filtering out the most qualitative of them and making sure that they get the support and funding that they need?	☐ YES ☐ NO
CREATIVE CLIMATE	Nourishing an open, knowledge-sharing and creative climate	Do you have open forums for discussion about where the market is heading and what it means in terms of innovation needs and long-term opportunities for your company?	☐ YES ☐ NO
PERSONAL COMMITMENT	Having people committed to bringing in new ideas and to supporting innovation	Does everyone in your company consider it part of their job to contribute to innovation, and do their managers openheartedly welcome ideas from the floor?	☐ YES ☐ NO

7

IT TAKES TWO TO TANGO

This is not a corporate culture dominated by bean counters, risk-avoiding lawyers, or design committees whose negotiated compromises inevitably lead to boring products and mediocrity. It's a culture that's comfortable with using the words 'passion' and 'excellence' in everyday conversation.

Christine Thompson – former Apple employee – about Apple's culture[1]

Out of a hundred people (in Sweden, I have to add), how many do you think would say that they have their dream job? And in which industries/sectors (Sweden again) do you think that these people work? The answers in Figure 7.1 were part of the 2010 outcome in *Manpower Work Life*[2] – an ongoing study of the changing work life that we are performing in Sweden and Norway in cooperation with one of the most future-ambitious recruitment and workforce outsourcing firms.

At the top we find creative, knowledge-oriented jobs with a great deal of independence – culture and media people, people in management positions and craftsmen – while the bottom of the pile consist of jobs with very few degrees of freedom. These jobs are also normally less paid. Even though

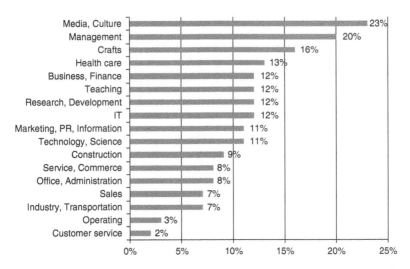

Figure 7.1 Share of employees thinking that they're currently in their dream job, by industry

sociologists have known for decades that salary isn't the top priority for most people, pay is still important: not because it makes us more committed or happy at work, but because pay that's not considered fair will make us start looking for greener grass. For instance, *Manpower Work Life* showed in 2010 that 22 percent of people switching jobs do so because they want a higher salary. According to this study, only 'greater challenges' are a stronger motive than pay for finding a new job.

WHAT'S A GOOD JOB?

So what else separates a good job from a bad one? In our *Global Values*[3] project in 2007 we asked 24,000 people in 17 countries about, among other things, work and work life. The most commonly stated characteristics of a good job (out of approximately 20 alternatives) in a selection of those countries are listed in Table 7.1.

Table 7.1 The traits of a good job according to people in different countries

SWEDEN	UK	FINLAND	GERMANY	FRANCE	SPAIN
Nice colleagues	Interesting and meaningful work	Interesting and meaningful work	Healthy working environment	Interesting and meaningful work	Employment security
Interesting and meaningful work	Pride in my job	Nice colleagues	Interesting and meaningful work	Pride in my job	Nice colleagues
A good boss	Healthy working environment	A good boss	Employment security	Healthy working environment	Healthy working environment
Pride in my job	Employment security	Healthy working environment	Nice colleagues	Employment security	Pride in my job
Healthy working environment	A good boss	Ability to influence my working conditions	Pride in my job	A good boss	Good career prospects
Right to parental leave	Good career prospects	Pride in my job	A good boss	Good career prospects	Right to parental leave

POLAND	RUSSIA	USA	CHINA	JAPAN	TAIWAN
Interesting and meaningful work	Interesting and meaningful work	Pride in my job	Healthy working environment	Interesting and meaningful work	Healthy working environment
Employment security	High salary	Employment security	Good career prospects	Healthy working environment	Nice colleagues
A good boss	Good career prospects	Good benefits	Ability to influence my working conditions	Nice colleagues	A good boss
High salary	Healthy working environment	Healthy working environment	Nice colleagues	Good benefits	Employment security
Nice colleagues	To feel proud of my job	Interesting and meaningful work	Interesting and meaningful work	Employment security	Good career prospects
Pride in my job	A good boss	A good boss	Good benefits	A good boss	Good benefits

As you can see, with few exceptions the list turns out to be quite similar all over the world. However, anyone who has ever had an 'interesting and meaningful' job knows that interesting and meaningful isn't going to be enough in the long run. The problem is that what seemed to be interesting to start with will end up boring pretty soon if nothing happens. There needs to be development, progression and a feeling of future. If not, the talented with options will move and you'll end up with the rest: the least committed but yet fairly satisfied, and maybe even a few alienated who have already given up but value employment security highly.

THE IMPORTANCE OF KEEPING YOUR TEAM HAPPY

Of course, the end goal might not be that everyone is satisfied at work – and shouldn't be so either. From a management perspective, commitment is normally more important than mere satisfaction. However, how you feel at work tends to color other parts of your life. If you feel bad at work you tend to feel bad in life as a whole too, and if you feel bad at work and in life you normally want to do something about it. In this case *something* often means finding a new job. In one of our global studies, 46 percent of the alienated are currently looking for new jobs, compared with only 11 percent of the motivated. Thus, if you want to keep your team, you need to keep it happy.

Figure 7.2 is based on a weighted sample of middle-aged people from six European countries – the Scandinavian countries, Finland, Spain and France – and comes from a study in 2006 that we called *Generation Ambition*.[4] Among other things, we studied how job satisfaction varied as a function of influence, commitment and affirmation. What *Generation Ambition* revealed in this matter is how crucial it

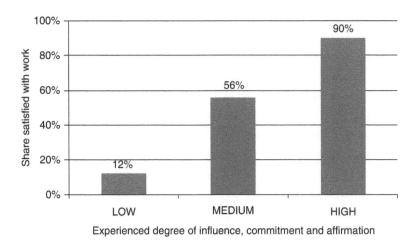

Figure 7.2 Work satisfaction as a function of influence, commitment and affirmation

is to deliver the bits and pieces that make people happy at work. If you don't, almost nobody will be happy. If you do, almost everyone will.

ENGAGEMENT: THE ORGANIZATIONAL GOLDEN EGG

During the global research project that gave me the inspiration to write this book we found that successful teamwork is built on engagement. Determined people are those who are satisfied and committed at work, those who *drive* the business, so it's really important to have such people onboard. Engagement is the most important resource in any organization, and if it fades, you're in serious trouble.[5] But what motivates people? What makes us get up in the morning, come to work, feel committed and satisfied? And what can you do as a manager to improve engagement? That's what I want to talk to you about. In this section, we explore what engagement consists of and how it can be nourished.

A generation of mercenaries

In one global company we worked with, 60 percent of the 30-year-olds were motivated, compared with 70 percent for those 20 years older. So why are young people less engaged? Is it because they're more frustrated or even alienated – perhaps because they haven't yet found their perfect place to be? Yes, but not primarily. The primary reason is that they're less committed. They like their job, but are less committed to it than their older workmates. And this is nothing unique for this firm. Young people today have more of a mercenary approach to work and sign up for whoever pays best (and pay can mean anything from money to development opportunities). Instead of seeing themselves as lifelong servants, young people are temporary visitors on their way to the next gig.[6]

Young people today consider work to be nothing more than a contract, which results in a sometimes close to non-existent loyalty. They're more in it for the fun, as a part of which they like to bring their friends to work – perhaps not in flesh, but through their social networks. And importantly (which we'll get back to): they're not willing to trade life for work. When young people are looking for a new job, they're more interested in workmates and working hours than they are in the quality of the products and services. As a consequence, it's no longer enough to provide good working conditions. For engagement, most organizational characteristics have become hygiene factors, meaning that they're no longer plus-factors, only minus factors: lack of them is demotivating. It's not even enough that work provides a nice experience, that it's fun and interesting. It's the transformational power, the me-making capacity of a workplace that makes the difference.

From we-making to me-making – and back again

Values researchers across the globe have been tracking increasing individualization for decades. In brief, people are turning to *me-making* activities rather than *we-making* ones. More than ever before, people are looking for social contexts in which their personal benefit is a transformed self: *a better me.*[7] In work life, for instance, we're chasing experience and personal development – the me-aspects of work. And this is especially true for younger and more highly educated people.

The shift from *we* to *me* challenges traditional organizations. But what characterizes organizations with the ability to attract the me-oriented young talent? In short it seems that the me-making capacity is a product of at least three things: the ambitions and actions of the manager and the composition of the team and its tasks. In fact, research shows that in order to attract and keep your employees – especially the well-educated, young, highly motivated and me-oriented ones – a dynamic, talented and ambitious team is critical.[8] Similarly, managers who get high scores from subordinates seem to be better at creating such a positive culture and team spirit. So, surprisingly, a sense of *we* seems to be more critical than ever to attracting me-making talents. And this somewhat paradoxical relationship indicates what's coming next.

In many industrialized economies, people born in the 1970s and 1980s are more individualistic and money-oriented when they enter the labor market than those born in the 1960s or earlier were. This is essentially the root of the ongoing shift from *we* to *me*. However, like many other things, such attitudes and preferences move in cycles, as illustrated in Figure 7.3.[9] What we can expect from the

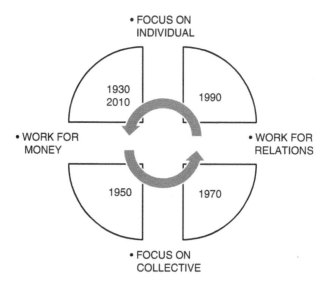

Figure 7.3 Attitudes and preferences of young people over the decades

next generation of employees is therefore possibly a steady decline in individualism, already manifested through the increasingly central role of team spirit. Relationships will become more important over the next decades, and a we-making culture similar to that of the postwar era can be expected by the time the now newborns enter the labor force.

What makes people dance

But if we don't want to wait for times to change, can we somehow convert young people to commitment today? Well, believe it or not, young people are almost like old guys. That means that what motivates people in general also motivates the young. An energizing work environment is attractive, no matter your age. Study after study shows that young people are constantly seeking excitement, fun, development and freedom at work. By concentrating on that, you can develop a truly attractive workplace for both young and old. Because even though there's no *one-strategy-fits-all* to finding out what makes each and every one of your employees tick, of course, engagement is not rocket science. It's more common sense as it has very much to do with basic human needs. In short, there are five drivers of engagement, which I usually illustrate as an engagement tree like the one in Figure 7.4.

In a high-performing company, how many people do you think manage to climb to the highest branch? Our research tells us that it's about one out of four, or 25 percent. Among those, nine out of ten feel engaged. At the opposite end – among those who fail to feel any of the

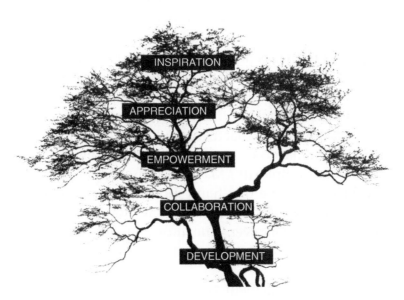

Figure 7.4 The Engagement tree[10]

desired emotions – only five percent feel motivated. A simple thing like appreciation is important to making people feel respected and valued at work, but also (as we've already seen) to make them stay. Appreciation is especially important for the old faithful workhorses: those who have been around for years, doing their job, but making no noise. They're the ones most likely not to feel appreciated, but rather forgotten. So, be explicit. Give people appreciation and recognition – even those that don't seem to need it. Because they do!

TALENT EXCELLENCE

In a survey that my company conducted in 2007, several hundred HR managers in Swedish corporations and government agencies were asked to pick key future competencies from a list of 30 alternatives, all suggested by HR mangers in dialogues and focus groups. What we found was that the most precious skill to possess in order to get a job in their companies ten years ahead is *the ability to deliver on time*. A similar study two years later also showed that when these HR managers hire fresh university graduates, the most critical but hard-to-find skill is *the ability to understand and manage complexity*. My guess is that these results are quite universal. So why do HR managers focus on such opposite competencies – delivery and complexity? Maybe because they're needed in a world that on the one hand moves more quickly than ever before, and on the other hand is more unpredictable and complex than ever. The most important question, however, is how to motivate and keep the ones that have these talents.

Employee engagement is closely related to the overall performance of the firm. A study of nine countries that we performed for the global ICT giant contained a ranking-system of factors related to the notion of being *talent excellent* – both in terms of the average effect of these factors on the organization's performance and, more specifically, their effects on employee engagement. In the following five sections we'll dig deeper into the most important of these cornerstones to find out how you and your organization can become truly talent excellent. What you can expect in return for your efforts in this area is high performance by committed employees who are easily attracted to and retained in the organization.

Ambitious team

One of the largest challenges ahead, as we move further into the Thought economy, is to find and retain talent. And since talent is attracted by talent and by a talent-oriented culture – characterized (shortly and partly) by goal-oriented teamwork with talented and ambitious colleagues – an ambitious team is the new *we-factor*. To keep commitment

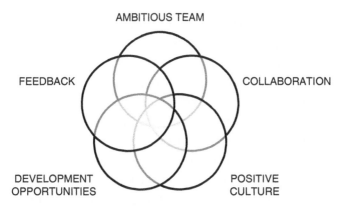

Figure 7.5 The cornerstones of talent excellence

on top is therefore the greatest challenge of all. However, being talented isn't a sufficient common denominator for successful teams, as one of our *Manpower Work Life* studies has shown. In fact, what's needed is a sense of belonging to the group – and that feeling emerges from common interests. In companies where a majority of team members have similar interests about 80 percent of employees say that they're working efficiently in a positive atmosphere, while only 50 percent of employees with no common interests say the same thing. Similarly, progressivity in work methods seems to follow common interests. So in order to get efficiency and progression from the team, the team-maker needs to create a team with a sense of affinity: a team in which people click.

Collaboration

Do you know what a search on your corporate website really says about you? Have you ever Googled your own name to see what your footprint on the Internet is? And are you, like many others, keeping track of your boss through social media? These sources of information are a vital source for everyone from employees to board members, clients and customers – and to people thinking about applying for a job at your firm. The *Manpower Work Life* study from 2010 showed that almost half of nearly 10,000 respondents – especially employees in knowledge industries and among those with university education – are checking out their future managers on the Internet. Why? Because having a smooth cooperation between people at different levels in the company starts and ends with management, and the most common reason people give for wanting to leave their jobs is because their boss sucks (excuse my English).

Our *Generation Ambition* study, in which employees in several countries including Sweden were asked to relate their propensity of quitting their jobs to how much they trusted their supervisor, showed that trust in your supervisor affects your propensity to scout for other employers. Forty-one percent of those planning to switch jobs have low trust in their supervisor, while the number for employees with high trust is only 15 percent. So clearly, managerial abilities are closely related to whether people consider finding other employment or not. Furthermore, the result from *Manpower Work Life* 2010 in Figure 7.6 shows that reliance in your manager constitutes an important part of whether you would consider recommending a friend with the right qualifications to apply for a job where you work or not.

So how do you gain your employees' trust? By trusting them back! Empowerment alone – having the authority to deal with problems at work – means more to engagement

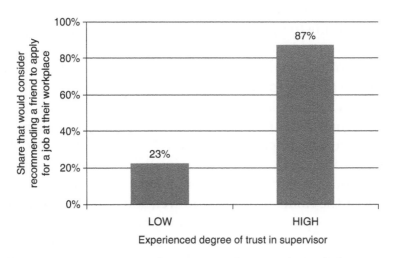

Figure 7.6 Propensity of recommending one's workplace as a function of trust in supervisor

than all managerial activities together. So, whatever you do as a manager, don't forget to give people a say. The simple advice here is: trust, encourage and never ever micromanage; it will pay off. According to our studies, often around 60 percent of your average team members feel empowered, and they are much more engaged than your other employees. Since empowerment is essentially a newcomer or young talent issue as employees that have been with the team for a while normally feel more empowered than those who just arrived, you should put extra energy into the novices. As a bonus, leadership that is empowering and builds on collaboration significantly increases the understanding of the supervisor's situation, which tends to increase the confidence in his or her actions too.

Positive culture

But why is corporate culture so important? Well, simply because the nature of the corporate culture is what everyone is trying to figure out before they apply for a job. Apart from the products and services that primarily make you proud of the company you work for, it's the culture that you are looking for. In 2010, the *Manpower Work Life* study asked what people look at before deciding to apply for a job. What we found is that corporate culture and hours of work are very important. Figure 7.7 shows that for people already in employment and especially in knowledge-based jobs, the boss matters almost as much as the corporate culture or the hours of work. However, some industries stand out: for people in healthcare, customer service, warehousing, services and industrial work – all of them employment with relatively few degrees of freedom – the hours of work are the central issue.

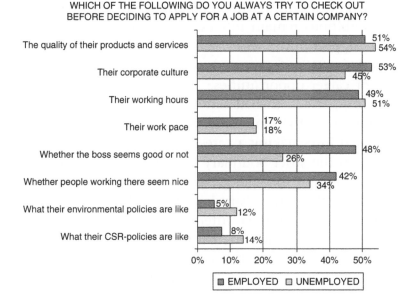

WHICH OF THE FOLLOWING DO YOU ALWAYS TRY TO CHECK OUT
BEFORE DECIDING TO APPLY FOR A JOB AT A CERTAIN COMPANY?

Figure 7.7   What people try to find out about a workplace before applying for a job

So it isn't merely due to its interesting and successful products that Google receives roughly one million job applications every year. The perception of Google as a company with a fun, open and innovative corporate culture – manifested in benefits including everything from game rooms, gourmet restaurants and sports facilities to massage, dry-cleaning and carwashing, to mention a few – is just as important. And having a positive and energizing corporate culture where people have fun has clearly paid off – at least in the Google case.

Development opportunities

The greatest challenge to small, knowledge-intensive organizations is to create good development and career opportunities within the company so that the talented and ambitious remain interested instead of searching for these opportunities elsewhere. According to *Manpower Work Life 2010*, 56 percent leave their employers due to a lack of career opportunities. These opportunities tend to vanish especially in bad times, and especially for young employees. At the same time, young people don't want to be forced into making a career when the times are good. Although the strict boundary between life and work isn't very prominent for younger generations, the integrity of one's spare time and leisure is sacred to them.

In a recent study we interviewed 500 managers with team members in their 20s *and* 1000 of their 20-something employees, comparing their views on managing young people. Among the young, constant personal and professional development was the top priority,[11] and this strong drive challenges managers and organizations. While managers need to shift from being managers to becoming trainers, focusing on the personal and professional development of their team members, organizations need to be redesigned as "boot camps".[12] And, consequently, the HR-function needs to start focusing on talent development rather than talent attraction.

But let us return to the work-life-balance issues that for a decade have been a priority in many industries. The general trend is that the role of work in the everyday lives of most people is becoming smaller. In 2005, I conducted a study of future leaders and the problems and opportunities of recruiting leaders.[13] One hypothesis we went in with was that it would be hard to find enough young people to replace the baby boomers when they leave work. Surprisingly, that seemed not to be the case. Seventy-six percent of the then 30–35 year old Swedes that were interviewed said that they

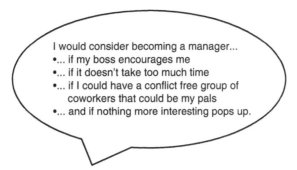

Figure 7.8   The buts of becoming a manager

could consider becoming a manager, and half of those, or 38 percent, said that they 'definitely' could consider that. There was just one (or in realty several) *but(s)*: 'I have to be able to have a life'.

What 'having a life' means differs quite a lot between nationalities, though. Figure 7.9 comes from our *Global Youth*[14] project and presents the choices that 16–29 year olds make. Finland is in its own league, with 45 percent of its young saying that they prefer a stimulating but demanding job. At the other end of the scale, Taiwan stands out, with 57 percent saying that they definitely want jobs with clear boundaries. So is this a reflection of different attitudes and priorities in general, or is it rather a reflection of the labor market in different countries? The fact that also Japan, USA, Spain and China are in the bottom speaks for the latter – or at least we can assume that the local context highly influences the respondent's answers. None of these countries are famous for their long vacations or short days.

Another interesting cultural difference exists in the attitudes of managers towards their own position. While 75 percent of Swedish managers say that they like leading

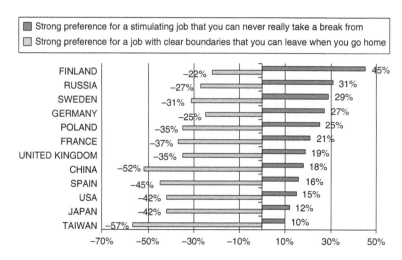

Figure 7.9 Cultural differences in work-life-balance preferences

others, the same number for Spanish managers is only 51 percent. And while 90 percent of US managers think that the work they perform as managers is important, only 60 percent of French managers agree.[15] Managers in the US and in Spain are more sacrificial than most: almost a fifth of them would rather *not* be a manager if it were up to them. In Sweden and France, that's only true for every twentieth manager. So as we can see, it's crucial to keep track of employee career interests – especially if your team works in several countries or is otherwise multicultural. Forcing someone to advance might be just as harmful to the team as preventing another from climbing.

Feedback

The tango idiom in the title of this chapter was chosen for a reason: both successful teamwork and this dance rely on close interaction between leaders and followers.

Just like the employer-employee relationship, tango is both close and improvisational; both dancers need to be excellent at their roles as they move in relation to each other – sometimes in the same direction and sometimes in opposition. What managers can learn from tango dancers is how important dynamic interaction is. Teamwork is about giving and taking, and this applies to feedback and conflict management too. And in my experience, this is where far too many managers fail.

According to our nine-country study of performance drivers, more than 25 percent of the employees in many organizations say that inefficient organization is a barrier to operational excellence in their firms. In short, there are three roots of inefficiency: unclear work processes and structure, unclear targets and directions and unclear communication. Such inefficiencies have a negative impact on performance, as seen in Figure 7.10, which originates from the nine-country study. The relationship between clear targets and high performance is easy to spot: almost 80 percent of companies in which the average team says it's working with clear targets are high-performers, while just over only a few percent of the companies with less clear targets are.

To make matters worse, lack of clarity isn't just a barrier to operational excellence. In fact, the indirect effects of lack of clarity might be even worse than the direct effects. Most of us know this from experience: while clear targets and communication can deliver lust, inspiration and enthusiasm, hassle is the ultimate lust-killer. Inefficient organization and unclear roles and responsibilities are the two strongest drivers of 'lack of inspiration in daily work' according to several studies we've performed. If you kill inspiration through an inefficient and unclear organization, you'll also kill engagement and eventually the business itself, because

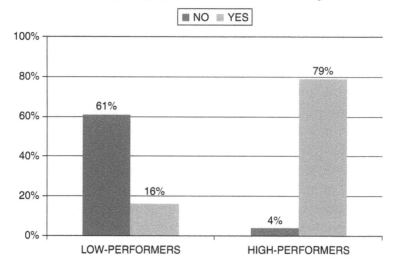

Figure 7.10 The relation between overall performance and clarity

inspiration is the very root of the Engagement tree. That's the main reason why removing hassle is a key factor not only to short-term performance but also to long-term success. Inspiration is about feeling a spirit and enthusiasm in daily work. It's about having fun, but fun is volatile. The greatest threat to fun is bureaucracy, rivalry and conservatism, so kill those and inspiration will sky rocket!

As a manger it's important to remember that it's better to focus on removing obstacles and inconveniences as quickly as possible than try to build a perfect organization – simply because there's no such thing as a perfect organization. There'll always be inefficiency, conflicts and inconveniences, so the trick is to get rid of the worst parts as quickly as possible and try to prevent them from coming back. Organizational research tells us to start with the easy ones from the top, the most obvious ones: efficiency in processes and clarity in structure. Normally, that's where the low-hanging fruits are, the obstacles that cause the greatest trouble and the problems that are the most easily solved. If the problems remain, you can always continue to the next level. So if you want to focus on the basics, do the following:

- **Make hassle-reduction a top priority.** Make processes as simple as possible and ensure that nothing is preventing people from doing their job. Enforce organizational clarity as far as possible, not only for the sake of operational excellence, but also for the sake of engagement.

- **Focus on targets and tasks.** When the whole team is dancing to the same tune the difficulties that are bound to appear over time won't necessarily have to slow down productivity. By focusing on targets and tasks you'll prevent many problems from occurring.

- **Watch out for poor communication.** As soon as something is unclear or rivalry occurs, make it the number one priority. For this mechanism to function when things go south, employer–employee feedback needs to be a mutual and well-rehearsed part of the everyday agenda.

DANCING WITH THE TEAM

Self-assessment is the first step towards succeeding in the T-economy. Are you prepared to climb the Engagement tree in the me-making jungle?

CORNERSTONE	MEANING	ARE YOU FIT FOR THE FUTURE?	ASSESSMENT
AMBITIOUS TEAM	Feeling part of a talented, ambitious and goal-oriented team	Is the exchange of knowledge and experience between colleagues a major factor in why people want to work in your company?	☐ YES ☐ NO
COLLABORATION	Cooperating smoothly with and being empowered by managers and teammates	Do employees in your company encourage their friends to apply for jobs there?	☐YES ☐ NO
POSITIVE CULTURE	Having a positive and energizing work culture where people support and have fun	Is there a shared vision for the team as to what you want to deliver, and is the team energized by working together towards these goals? Do team members have fun together?	☐ YES ☐ NO
DEVELOPMENT OPPORTUNITIES	Adapting career opportunities to individual goals and private life situations	Do the most ambitious and talented of your colleagues stay in the company instead of searching for opportunities elsewhere?	☐ YES ☐ NO
FEEDBACK	Having a strong feedback culture based on efficient and clear dialogue	Do people in your team actively and continuously seek feedback from each other?	☐ YES ☐ NO

138

8

DANCING CHEEK-TO-CHEEK

It's all about passion, stupid!

In the field of B2B- and B2C-relations, three trends are shaping the landscape. These might be called customer deficit, commodization and transformation. The first trend – customer deficit – is what it is: lack of customers. In most markets, in most industries and most parts of the value chain there's a production overcapacity that is creating a buyers' market. The customer deficit leads to the second trend – commodization – as unique products and services don't survive for long in vicious price competition. Undifferentiated products and services are traded on commodity markets, where personal sales are rapidly replaced by more or less automated transaction sales. At the same time, what customers are looking for is related to the third trend: transformation. The power of a product, service or relationship to offer self-fulfillment and change through consumption is, in some sense, the ultimate value to the customer whose basic needs have already been attended to.

In the raw material era described in Chapter 3 most companies delivered undifferentiated commodities, and consequently extracting and trading those raw materials and commodities were what business was about. Entering the production era of the 18th and 19th centuries, companies went into industrial production and (later) services. At the end of the 20th century, expectations – not least from end consumers – shifted towards *experiences*, illustrated by extreme price differentiation in most trades. Salt, for instance, could cost one or a hundred dollars per kilo, depending on how it was extracted and presented. Western societies became more and more experience-based, where even work itself became an experience as younger generations at least expected to have fun at work.

As we recently moved into the prime of the production era, not even experiences were enough anymore. To deliver real value you now needed to provide *transformation*. In the field of B2B-sales, transformation became what differentiated valuable services from commoditized ones, and consumer markets soon followed suit. Individuals were now looking for change and development, so consumer industries got into the business of marketing transformation too. The increasing demand for personal trainers and plastic surgeons is a result of this. However, we again seem to be moving into new demands. Our research shows that customers are now seeking *togetherness*, or at least that togetherness is what makes experiences really valuable.[1] Already, this development has meant great business for the travel industry. Figure 8.1[2] comes from one of our recent reports in Swedish (developed for Parks and Resorts, Scandinavia's leading entertainment park owner) and illustrates the evolution towards higher degrees of uniqueness and customer value.

The search for togetherness perhaps even explains the partner-seeking trend in B2B-sales, viewed in light of the search for long-term relations and co-development. A business relationship in which both parties' dreams of transformation are fulfilled could be likened to a couple-dance where the partners both take turns leading and following,

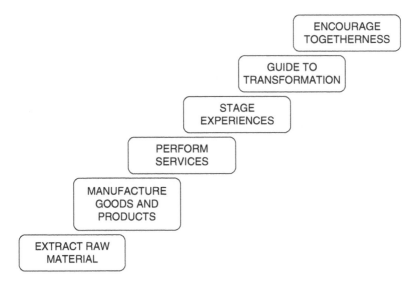

Figure 8.1   The evolution of economic value

because although following your client, customer or partner is necessary, it's not enough. To be able to provide true
value, you also have to be able to lead, and propose new
ideas, solutions and directions based on in-depth insights
into the customer's business and what provides value
to their customers. So whether you're a B2B- or a B2C-
company, and whether you deliver services or products,
doesn't matter. The success factors remain the same: customer intimacy, emotional links and joint innovation.

SALES EXCELLENCE

So what is it that makes customers dance? That certainly
depends on both the industry and the customer. Some
clients are easy to please while others aren't. However, in
the research we've performed over the last decade, we've
found six factors to be especially correlated with mean

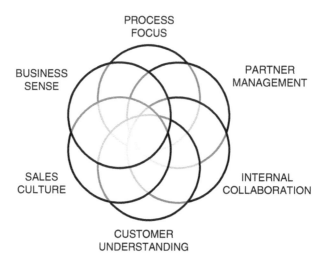

PROCESS
FOCUS

BUSINESS
SENSE

PARTNER
MANAGEMENT

SALES
CULTURE

INTERNAL
COLLABORATION

CUSTOMER
UNDERSTANDING

Figure 8.2 The cornerstones of sales excellence

performance. The remainder of this chapter is arranged around these six cornerstones, listed in Figure 8.2 in clockwise order of importance, starting at noon. What we can immediately see is that sales excellence doesn't only have to do with sales directly, but has much deeper roots into the organization. As an example, both process focus and internal collaboration often are more important to the company's mean sales performance than the sales culture itself.

Process focus

The most important factor behind successful sales is process focus, which may seem a bit odd. But good products and sales talk will only take you so far, and the skills of the salesperson say less about a company's sales performance than the practices implemented in the organization and its culture. So it's not so much about who your salespeople are (although that's important too, of course) but rather about the processes that those salespeople follow.

In order to take customers from *leads* to long-term partnerships, well-defined and applied processes are needed. Customer-centric organizations constantly find new ways to work with the clients, making them feel unique. In return, they receive input into new innovations and customer loyalty. The payoff is obvious when comparing process-focused firms to others, as in Figure 8.3: firms that that apply a systematic approach to client generation, development and retention simply perform better.

Partner management

As clients become global and partnership relations tighten, the pressure on suppliers to deliver a broader spectrum of

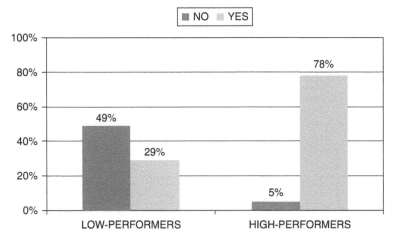

'We have a well-defined and applied process that covers the whole chain from lead generation to developing long-term customer relations'

Figure 8.3 The relation between overall performance and process focus

products and services over wider geographical areas grows. To be able to do that, you need partners on the supplier side: companies with whom you join forces in order to serve the market and your key customers. Thus, the road to customer intimacy is linked with another road of intimacy, namely partner intimacy. At the same time it's not just customer intimacy that drives the need for stronger relations on the supply-side – so too do increasing customer demands. In an study of B2B-companies that we performed in 2005, 73 percent said that expectations on suppliers are getting higher.[3] And increasing customer expectations isn't in any way unique to the B2B-industry. It's just as valid for consumer industries. Over the past decades, customer expectations have been rapidly increasing while the tolerance for mistakes or deviations in quality have decreased at a similar pace, as illustrated in Figure 8.4.

The New World doesn't just mean higher market expectations. Turning from simpler buyer-supplier relations to more complex partnerships also asks more of the supplier

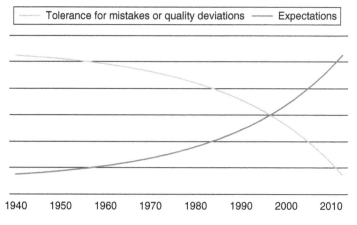

Figure 8.4 Modern markets demand a lot of its participants

in terms of complexity management. In the most developed form of cooperation, the supplier becomes a business partner and the salespeople business developers, supporting the partner with an intricate mix of products and services. Therefore, the ability to manage complex networks of partners and suppliers in joint client projects becomes increasingly important as clients ask for more intimate and caretaking relationships.

Internal collaboration

So how do you achieve successful partner management? What kind of requirements do customer intimacy, increasing expectations and higher complexity pose on the supplying company? In short, the answer is 'Work as one!' The more complex your business relationships are (that is, the more contact points you have with your client and the wider the range of services and products you supply), the more important is internal collaboration. The reason is simple: The front people of your organization, responsible for the business relationship, need to know that they have full backup. As soon as a problem surfaces it has to be dealt with. In some of the most efficient companies I have worked with, there are direct hotlines between the key accounts of major clients and the regional CEOs or even the global R&D departments so that if a client runs into trouble with a service or function, the problem is dealt with straightway. An organization with good internal collaboration between sales and other parts of the organization not only provides maximum value to customers as their demands can be met swiftly and without struggle, but also improves the company's overall performance, as is seen in Figure 8.5.

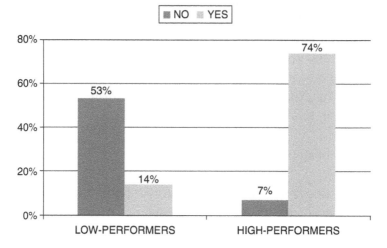

'Collaboration between units is fast, making it easy to respond quickly to customer demands'

Figure 8.5 The relation between overall performance and collaboration

Customer understanding

That customer understanding is key to sales success is obvious: without thorough customer understanding it's impossible to meet expectations. But customer understanding is about much more than just understanding the needs. Successful sales also require a thorough understanding of the decision-making processes in the client organization (who are involved, what are their priorities, and so on). Customer segmentation, stakeholder mapping and other activities are therefore central activities applied by successful sales organizations in the quest for the Nirvana of customer understanding. Just *how* important such activities are depends, however, on what you deliver and how strong your offers are compared to those of your competitors, which we'll look into in the last section of this chapter.[4]

Sales culture

Having a strong brand and outstanding products and offers is good because it makes sales a walk in the park. But there are companies that for long periods of time have built their success on far weaker offers, compensating for that weakness through having an outstanding sales culture. On the other hand there are plenty of companies with strong products and weak sales cultures, where sales is considered a *necessary evil* and where every truly professional member of the organization keeps his or her hands off sales. In those organizations sales are normally involved in a constant battle with other departments, and these companies are very far from the 'work-as-one' concept discussed above.

In our research we've of course also come across several companies with both strong products *and* outstanding sales cultures, one of them being the Swedish newspaper corporation Metro, which delivers free newspapers in 21 countries. During an interview, one of their executives gave a vivid illustration of what might be going on in a company with a strong sales culture. As the executive told it, one of their journalists was on his way back to the office when he passed a fashion shop with 'SALE' written all over the window. He looked in but found no customers, so he immediately picked up his phone, called the sales department and asked them to close a deal on an ad for tomorrow's edition. And that, my friends, is an excellent sales culture in action.

Business sense

Successful sales aren't just about fulfilling customers' dreams and desires. They are also about developing your

147

own company. Therefore, business sense is a critical part of sales excellence, and successful companies have managers who nurture it by communicating the need to focus on profitability, revenues and business opportunities.

An important part of applying business sense is choosing the right sales strategy based on the strength of the offers and the complexity of your products and services. The performance drivers discussed above play out differently in different contexts. Figure 8.6 schematically shows how. With complex product- and service-portfolios, stronger partner relations and no specific competitive advantage in terms of quality or brand, customer understanding is the most critical factor. In such businesses the sales culture is therefore relatively more important than in environments with more or less unique products and single product or service offers. For businesses with few but strong offers the

Figure 8.6 A plan of action guided by the strength and complexity of your offer

best way forward is instead to move as rapidly as possible, to harvest when there's still time.

DANCING WITH CUSTOMERS

Self-assessment is the first step towards succeeding in the T-economy. Are you prepared to strive towards the Nirvana of customer understanding and services?

CORNERSTONE	MEANING	ARE YOU FIT FOR THE FUTURE?	ASSESSMENT
PROCESS FOCUS	Applying a customer perspective to take clients from leads to partnership	Do you have a systematic process in place? Is it customer-centric and does it support and enhance the performance of your salespeople?	☐ YES ☐ NO
PARTNER MANAGEMENT	Managing complex networks of partners and suppliers in joint projects	Do you have a network of partners and suppliers that can help you meet your customers' expectations and needs, and are you in pole position in that network?	☐ YES ☐ NO
INTERNAL COLLABORATION	Collaborating with sales and other units to provide maximum value to customers	Does your entire organization work as one in order to give better offers and support to your customers and clients?	☐ YES ☐ NO
CUSTOMER UNDERSTANDING	Understanding the customers' businesses and what provides added value to them	Do you understand your customers' businesses and needs better than they do themselves?	☐ YES ☐ NO
SALES CULTURE	Seeing, valuing and recognizing sales not as a necessary evil, but as a religion	Have any of your employees or teammates ever called in with a sales lead in their spare time? Are the sales peoples the heroes in your organization?	☐ YES ☐ NO
BUSINESS SENSE	Focusing on profitability, revenues, opportunities and on making business	Do you know how to play the game, considering the strength and complexity of your own and your competitors' business offers?	☐ YES ☐ NO

9

BUILDING THE JAMMING ORGANIZATION

> The future belongs to those companies that
> are masters of Aha!

Leading organizations is first and foremost about creating value. It's about making the organization stronger, richer and fitter, with better processes, products and offerings. A primary mission for a manager or leader is to leave the organization in a better shape than he or she received it in, and the purpose of this book is to provide some guidelines on what to think about in that process. In the first part of the book I outlined the characteristics of the emerging business landscape under the headline of *The T-economy*, while in the second part I have introduced some of the performance drivers in that economy. In this final chapter, the ambition is to put it all together into an integrated framework for how to turn your business into a jamming organization: a value-creating entity fit for the future.

THINKING, LINKING AND BLINKING IN THE T-ECONOMY

As we saw in Chapter 3, the T-economy challenges companies to refocus from production and productivity to thinking and thought productivity (or to producing as many *Aha!s* per time unit as possible). The thought cell is the new factory and the thought net the new distributed production system. Information, ideas and intellectual property are the new raw materials and business or product concepts the new products. We also noticed that linking (meaning the process of networking and connecting to critical information nodes) is a critical value that creates process in a world where access to new fresh ideas is key to success. Finally, we saw that thinking and linking isn't enough. You still have to *blink* as well – to zoom out, see the big picture, trust your gut feeling and find your Kairos-moment, your defining moment. The last is definitely easier said than done.

In a few lines, the summary above recaps what running a T-company is about. It illustrates how value is created in the T-economy through two lines of action: the market line and the organizational line or, in other words, through *thought-driven market attractiveness* and *thought effectiveness and productivity*. How that could be done is what we will discuss in this chapter.

21ST CENTURY LEADERSHIP: BUILDING FUTURE CAPITAL

During the heydays of the industrial era, creating corporate value was mainly about money, and companies were valued according to their tangible assets. Today, market value is about future assets: the expectation of future market success and dividends. However, not only market value is based on the future. The foundation of *real* corporate value, the value a leader would love to hand over to the next generation of leaders, is also about *Future Capital* in terms of:

■ **Future products and offerings.** Products, patents and brands that are *fit for the future*. Tangible assets that can be traded in a market.

■ **Future capabilities.** Culture, processes and posture that make the organization resilient and capable of producing new streams of innovation. These capabilities are less tangible, and are thus hard to copy and trade.

Over the last 20 years I've been involved in hundreds or even thousands of client projects dealing with future challenges, trends and strategies. Experiences from those projects, in combination with several research projects as well as real-life experiences from both the corporate and the government and NGO worlds, have convinced me that this is what leadership in the 21st century is basically all about. What I've also learned is that it all has to start with a clear view of where the market and business context is heading. Management in today's turbulent world needs first and foremost to be *future-centric* and *thought-driven*. It is no longer enough to be customer-centric, although it is of course necessary to understand the customer's needs and expectations. You need to be able to understand where your customers are heading – what their *future* expectations will be – even before they know that themselves. And more often than you like, you will not be able to find out what the next big thing might be by simply asking your customers. You will have to invent the future yourself, and to do so you need to be both future-centric and thought-driven.

So focusing on your future market, your future products and offerings, your future capabilities and organization: that's where you have to start if you want to increase the *real value* of your organization and not just temporarily improve its dividends. But while prospering for a few years is relatively easy, building long-term value is harder but far more important in the long run. The question is: do you understand the challenges ahead – and have you got what it takes to cope with them?

So, to approach this Grand Challenge you must first understand your future challenges and opportunities in the market, as well as your organization's ability to face the challenges and profit from the opportunities. In Figure 9.1 I've called this Future Capability Analysis and Future Market Analysis.

Building internal Future Capital is, as we have seen in the previous chapters, critical to long-term success. For example, it's not enough for a great company like Apple to rely on one person's ability to capture implicit needs and desires and transpose them to outstanding products. The defining test of Steve Jobs' leadership ability comes now, as we're about to find out whether he was able to build a culture that could survive him or not.

A part of the Future Capability Analysis might be carried out as an integrative segment of the employee

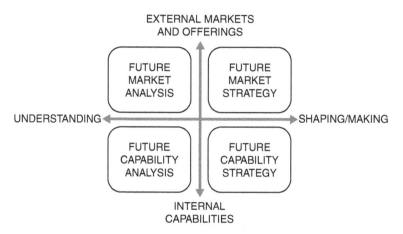

Figure 9.1 The four aspects of a Future Capital process

survey. Introducing questions that capture real performance drivers – such as the ones we've been discussing in
Chapters 5–8 – alongside traditional questions focusing
employee satisfaction and (more lately) employee engagement provides a clear view of what to focus on in order
to improve future-making capabilities. Employee survey
data can also be linked to performance data on customer
satisfaction, organic growth or other key performance
indicators available at the unit level. The Future Capability Analysis is essential in defining the Future Capability
Strategy, but also important in developing the Future
Market Strategy.

Understanding the future market is often harder than
we think. Looking far into the future usually helps since
it makes it easier to let go of the present, to see the big
picture and the long-term consequences of megatrends
with high impact on the industry and on organizational
capabilities. The key question is: what will the industry
look like in three, five, ten or even 20 years, and what does
it take to succeed in that context? (For a more in-depth
description on how to do that in practice, see for instance
Scenario planning – the link between future and strategy, written by myself and by one of my long-time colleagues, Hans
Bandhold.)

Analyzing the future business context gives you clues
about what to focus on, where the future hunting grounds
are, and where the future threats and risk are located.
The analysis provides a foundation for the Future Market
Strategy – the long-term strategy defined by the future
premises identified – and outlines what future markets,
new product categories and technologies you should
invest in, given the long-term trends and uncertainties in
the market.

FUTURE CAPABILITY CAPITAL

Some of the more universal, internal performance drivers in the T-economy have been examined in the previous chapters. We have discussed issues such as insight, change, innovation, talent and sales, and what the prime performance drivers within those fields are. But what are the intangibles that characterize the greatest companies and organizations? Is it even possible to point to just a few general characteristics? Judging from the research I have conducted with my colleagues, I think it is. And these characteristics can be summarized in just three words: *culture*, *processes* and *posture*.

In Chapter 6 we saw the application of these three dimensions in the field of innovation. We talked about the creative culture, about the supporting processes of customer and user understanding and about implementation capability. The same three dimensions – culture, processes and posture – occur in almost any field when one looks for the core performance drivers. An open, innovation-oriented and diverse culture is the foundation of a successful T-economy organization. But culture itself isn't the prime performance driver. It's a necessary but not sufficient prerequisite that has to be supported by and transformed into supporting processes in order to make a change. For instance, it's great to have an ongoing discussion about the changing business landscape – but *talking* about the future is usually quite far away from actually *making* it. Processes and practices, however, help narrow that gap.

Transforming culture into established and implemented processes and procedures makes the fluid and intangible culture more tangible. It's easier to introduce new recruits into established practices than to make them understand how the organization works without formalized procedures. Processes therefore make growth easier and definitely build value for the future. On the other hand, processes without entrepreneurial action are nothing more than bureaucracy. It's also impossible to keep a creative and open culture if the decision-making processes aren't in line with the organizational culture. Thus, a posture characterized by speed, braveness and willingness to get to the future first is what typifies the winners in the T-economy.[1]

Realizing the three levels of T-economy drivers affects leadership and management. In order to drive a creative and open culture you need empowering and listening leaders. However, strength at the level of processes requires much more of a tight and directive leadership, where setting and following up goals are key characteristics. Finally, the posture dimension requires visionary, innovative and even provocative leaders who are passionate about the long-term picture and dedicated enough to make it happen.

Balancing the organizational brain

There are, as we've just seen, three levels of Capability Capital: culture, processes and posture. Future-capable organizations are of course strong in all three dimensions, but what also characterizes them is that they're balanced. They don't just innovate, but also sell. They're don't just deal with long-term futures, but also develop an attractive organization in which people can grow today. In short, we could say that they're good at *both* running the business *and* at the same time changing it. If we combine the three levels of capabilities with the five performance drivers discussed earlier – insight, change, innovation, talent and sales – we realize that talent and sales are more strongly related to the operational side of

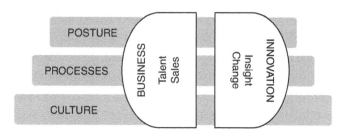

Figure 9.2 The internal capabilities that build Future Capital

the organization (the left hemisphere), while insight, innovation and change are more strongly related to the right hemisphere. Insight and change could also to some extent be said to be different aspects of innovation.

Using the popular metaphor of the human brain we could say that successful T-organizations manage both sides of the organizational brain (illustrated in Figure 9.2) well, and they succeed in keeping them together. Failing in the left hemisphere normally leads quite rapidly to red figures, while missing the right hemisphere leads to long-term failure. And organizational lobotomy ultimately means that the organization is unable to implement new ideas and concepts successfully.

FUTURE MARKET CAPITAL

In Chapter 6 we saw that the key performance drivers in many industries seem to be 'systematic processes for identifying new trends and opportunities in the market' and the ability to transform 'market insights into new products and offers'. Consequently, what could – based on those insights – be more important than building an *innovation machine*, the kind of machine discussed in Chapter 6? Such a machine would transfer knowledge about corporate performance drivers into what we just called Future Capability Capital, and in fact I've been developing such machines for our clients for over a decade. We call the model Trend and Innovation Management (TRIM) and believe it's the core concept of 21st-century management.

The TRIM-process – illustrated in Figure 9.3 – is quite simple and straightforward, and aims at easily making the often unplanned and unstructured innovative work that goes on in every organization more systematic and qualitative. The fundamental goal is to improve the speed and quality of innovation, meaning getting more and better ideas into the market or into new internal practices.

When initiating a TRIM-process, you first have to summarize your assumptions about the *key trends* and uncertainties in the market or field in which you are interested. Having a constantly updated Future Map is the first step to more future-oriented innovative moves, but makes

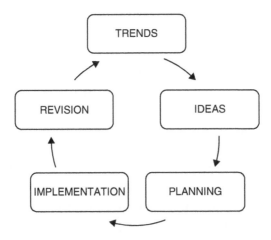

Figure 9.3 The Trend and Innovation Management Process (TRIM)

everyday decision-making easier too. From the trends, uncertainties or scenarios in the Future Map, one could start developing creative responses to medium- or long-term trends, challenges and opportunities. But not all such *ideas* could or should be implemented. Resources are scarce and many of the ideas not worth bringing forward. As Sofie Randén, Consumer Insight Manager at Kraft Foods Nordic and responsible for their TRIM-process, concludes: 'One of the greatest risks with trends is that there is an incredibly vast range of interesting information. With Kairos Future's trend management system you get help to focus on the most important trends for the organization and how they will affect the company, and create a concrete action plan to meet the upcoming changes in the best way.'[2]

Figures 9.4 and 9.5 illustrate some TRIM-process outcomes for Kraft Foods Nordic from the first half of the 2000s. Figure 9.4 is a snapshot of the Future Map that the company worked with one specific year, while Figure 9.5 illustrates some of the communicated results from the process. By applying simple ranking methods the most promising ideas – either market or processes related – could be selected and put into the *future portfolios*. This is the *planning* phase, but although planning sometimes has a value of its own, it normally needs to be followed by action to make a difference. For example, the launch of the successful Marabou Premium was a direct result of the identification of the trend 'everything goes premium' (discovered in another year from that illustrated in Figure 9.4). Spotting the trend and thinking hard about consequences and opportunities for each of Kraft Nordic's categories convinced the team that there was an opportunity to go for. With Marabou Premium, Kraft more or less created a

DEVELOPMENTS (UNCERTAIN)	TRENDS (LIKELY)	HOT ISSUES (CERTAIN)
• Personal touch • From product to cosmos • Digitalization of media • Show-room-effect	• New media & marketing logic • Retailers as market drivers • Conditional consumption • Safety in focus • Andromeda Galacticus • Booming Silver Generation • More mega mighty • Institutionalization • The emotional consumer • Migration of microcultures	• Hard discount shopping • Small indulgence • Public Health in focus • X-corporated manufacturing

Figure 9.4 Future Map by the Nordic division of Kraft Foods in the early 2000s

PROCESS RESULTS	SUCCESSFUL PRODUCT LAUNCHES
• Development of specific ideas • Support for new product launches • Development of new marketing concepts • Shared views of the future • Ability to select high-potential products from other markets • Improvement of existing products and ideas • Development of completely new concepts	• Marabou Premium – premium chocolate bars produced in different sizes. Immediate success and third best selling product within one year. • Estrella Gourmet – first premium chips in the Scandinavian market. • Low fat snacks – to cope with health trends.

Figure 9.5 Examples of outcomes from the Kraft Foods TRIM-process

market for premium chocolate in Scandinavia, where milk chocolate (and not least Marabou's own brand) previously reigned. Lastly, *implementation*, as well as assumptions and trends, needs to be subject to monitoring and *revision*.

The TRIM-model could be applied as an integrated part of the annual business planning, on either a corporate or unit level. Applying it as a day-to-day process, however, requires a more sophisticated approach than the one described above. Web-based supporting systems need to be added, procedures for the fast tracking of new ideas need to be developed, and so forth. Several of the clients we've helped implement a TRIM-process have also tailored the general concept to their specific needs.

As we've seen in the first three chapters of this book, the premises for market strategy and future mapping are rapidly changing. Applying thought leadership and a conscious focus on the future brings forward the ideas that result in new products entering the market, thus making the TRIM-process a tool for regaining control as the T-economy emerges. Over the years we've worked with numerous clients in all types of industries – from consulting and hospitality services to telecom, food and manufacturing industries – helping them gain thought leadership through systematic and continuous trend- and future-driven innovation processes. A well-managed TRIM-process has at least two advantages (beyond the obvious), namely reducing risk and providing control on the one hand, and improving speed and quality in the innovation process on the other. On top of that, a TRIM-process could be the vehicle for thought leadership in the industry or market, through the provision of knowledge and insight or through new innovative products and services.

FROM STRATEGY TO ACTION: THE FUTURE CAPITAL MODEL

Leading organizations is about creating real value or what we above have called Future Capital: a combination of Market

Capital (products, brands and patents fit for tomorrow's needs and desires as much as today's) and Capability Capital (organizations capable of benefiting from and adapting to the future), and *it all starts with an image*, a worldview, a big picture. Economist Kenneth Boulding concluded it already in 1956 in his seminal work *The Image*,[3] while his friend Fred Polak would have added an image 'of the future'.[4] I share the conclusion of Boulding and Polak, and as we've seen in the previous chapters there's a fair amount of recent research supporting us too. It all starts with an image of the future, and it *has to start* with such an *explicit* image because companies and leaders need to be explicitly future-centric.

The ambition of this final chapter was to put the different sections of the book together and to provide a working model for leadership in the 21st century. Two main conclusions can be drawn:

- **Leaders need to focus on shaping the future.** They need to be and employ future strategists, and they need to be future-centric.
- **Shaping the future requires roadmaps to navigate with.** Because if the leader gets lost, so will his or her followers.

Future strategist leadership

Leadership has always been about shaping the future. However, in times when the future comes in small doses, leaders need to be less future-oriented or future-centric than when the future goes for knockout. Today, and definitely so tomorrow, it goes for the knockout. Consequently, it is more important than ever to follow the old but still valid advice of Boulding and Polak – advice possibly even more valid than ever. Because getting started with the future or the big picture requires new skills. Therefore, managers and leaders need to be more strategic and externally oriented. They also need to be broader in scope, able to integrate both the various aspects of the changing business context and the organizational practices that build *real* corporate value. And they need to understand the interplay between external factors, organization and performance.

The time when top managers could stick to their own disciplines – be they finance, logistics or technology – is long gone. As a top-level manager you need to be broader and be able to understand the interlinked processes going on in the organization: how organizational practices interplay with customer satisfaction and brand perception, and how culture and proactivity drive innovation. As a leader and manager in the T-economy you need to be able to move freely between consumer understanding, employee motivation and leadership development, finance, change management, design, branding and R&D.

But no leader can be everything to everyone, and so companies therefore need to develop future-strategist functions and internal 'future-labs' with analysts as well as process leaders to assist top managers and leaders. In several surveys of the role of the business intelligence and strategy function in companies and large public sector organizations we have found that future strategists need to have a multi-disciplinary approach and be able not only to analyze the evolving business landscape and make wise conclusions, but also communicate insights and involve strategic decision-makers as well as the practitioners, experts and managers in the process.

The Future Capital Navigator

Shaping, making or winning the future requires a plan, but despite the complexity of the business landscape, successful strategies and plans normally need to be simple. One way to simplify strategy is to make an overview of all insights and activities linked to the strategy. We call that a Future Capital Navigator, and it summarizes the four parts of the Future Capital process described in this chapter:

- **Future Map.** A summary of the analysis regarding market context and internal future capabilities.

- **Strategy Map.** A summary of visions and strategic moves needed to develop Future Capital (Market and Capability Capital).

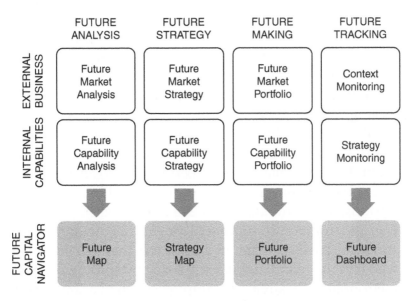

Figure 9.6 Setting up a Future Capital Navigator

- **Future Portfolio.** A portfolio of strategic actions, projects and investments based on the maps.

- **Future Dashboard.** A dashboard to keep track of the most relevant performance and project indicators and business context trends.

Figure 9.6 illustrates the relations between different planning activities discussed in the chapter and how they can be successfully compiled into such a navigator.

BUILDING A JAMMING ORGANIZATION

Around the turn of the last century I was busy summarizing the results of my doctoral work on strategy-related performance drivers in turbulent business environments. I had collected the data, made the interviews and performed the focus groups with top-level managers. I had the correlations and regression models. I knew that context awareness, cultural design and planning were important and that visionary proactivity and the willingness to win were separating the winners from the mediocre. What I was lacking was the story.

When I went through the material searching for metaphors in the literature, contextualizing the results once again, I realized that the high-performing organizations in what I today define as T-economy contexts function as jam sessions. Bertil Strandberg – the famous Swedish jazz musician and trombonist – once told me that 'if it doesn't swing, shoot the bassist'.[5] What he meant was that it's the bassist who lays the foundation for the swing by keeping the pace metronomic. Creativity and improvisation in a jam session relies on a foundation of structure built on metronomic pace and a shared understanding of the sequence of chords in the song played. Improvisation follows structure.

Great T-companies are organized as jam sessions, on a corporate level as well as on unit level. Structure and processes are the foundation of innovation and improvisation. The Future Capital Model is such a structure that, if well managed, could make your organization swing.

So put on your dancing shoes and get ready for dancing. And remember: it's all in the footwork!

NOTES

PREFACE

1. TAIDA stands for 'Tracking – Analyzing – Imaging – Deciding – Acting'. For a thorough description, see Lindgren, Mats and Bandhold, Hans, *Scenario Planning: The Link between Future and Strategy*, rev. and updated ed., Palgrave Macmillan, Basingstoke, 2009.
2. Development in the Eurozone during 2011 and the US subprime crisis in 2008 are only two of the most explicit examples of the 'closed-eyes strategy'.

INTRODUCTION

1. Personal correspondence with Theodore Modis, US business analyst, physicist and consultant. Based on an analysis of historical milestones, Modis has analyzed the increasing complexity. The results were presented in a couple of article. See for instance Modis, Forecasting the Growth of Complexity and Change, Technological Forecasting & Social Change, 69, No. 4, 2002.
2. This issue has been frequently reported. See for instance Foster, Richard N. and Kaplan, Sarah, *Creative Destruction: Why Companies that are Built to Last*

Underperform the Market, and how to Successfully Transform them, 1. ed., Currency/Doubleday, New York, 2001.

1   FRAGMENTS OF CHANGE

1. Eisenberg, Bryan, 'Hidden Secrets of the Amazon Shopping Cart', *FutureNow*, 26 February 2008, www.grokdotcom.com/2008/02/26/amazon-shopping-cart.
2. The quote has also been attributed to US dramatist Wilson Mizner (1876–1933).
3. September 2011, www.okcupid.com.
4. Kiron, David & Shockley, Rebecca, 'The New Intelligent Enterprise: Creating Business Value with Analytics', *MIT Sloan Management Review*, Sloan Management Review Association, Cambridge, MA, 2011.
5. See www.ted.com/talks/lang/eng/hans_rosling_shows_the_best_stats_you_ve_ever_seen.html.
6. These six minutes can be watched at www.ted.com/talks/lang/eng/gary_flake_is_pivot_a_turning_point_for_web_exploration.html.
7. Personal conversation.
8. See newsroom.husqvarna.com/category/global-garden-report for details.
9. Lorde, Audre and Hall, Joan W., *Conversations with Audre Lorde*, University Press of Mississippi, Jackson, 2004.
10. Whether this is exactly how We Feel Fine started is unknown. But lots of interesting information can be found at www.wefeelfine.org. You can also see Harris present We Feel Fine at www.ted.com/talks/jonathan_harris_tells_the_web_s_secret_stories.html.
11. Edgeworth, Francis Y., *Mathematical psychics: an essay on the application of mathematics to the moral*

sciences, London School of Economics and Political Science, London, 1932 [1881].

12. George MacKerron and Susana Mourato of the Department of Geography & Environment and the Grantham Research Institute on Climate Change and the Environment at the London School of Economics and Political Science (LSE).

13. Research results and much more are continuously published at blog.patientslikeme.com.

14. This quotation is commonly attributed to Mark Twain, although its origin hasn't been verified.

15. October 2010, www.kiva.org.

16. This quotation appears unaccredited.

17. Watch the clip at www.youtube.com/watch?v=5YGc 4zOqozo.

18. See, for example watch www.youtube.com/watch?v= tnOxvbGOTbM.

19. While the Hammonds and Setzer prank video has been banned from YouTube, CEO Patrick Doyle's response can be seen at www.youtube.com/watch?v=dem6eA7-A2I.

20. See www.adbusters.org.

21. © Erica Mann Jong, 1991, 2012, all rights reserved, used by permission of the poet. Jong, Erica, *Becoming Light: Poems New and Selected*, HarperCollins, New York, 1991.

22. One version of this story is written in Ferrari, Giulio, Ferrari, Mario & Hempel, Ralph, *Building robots with Lego Mindstorms: the ultimate tool for Mindstorms maniacs!*, Syngress Publ., Rockland, MA, 2002.

23. This quotation is commonly attributed to Oscar Wilde, although its origin hasn't been verified.

24. Read more about the case on Wikipedia or at hbswk. hbs.edu/archive/5258.html.

25. The *Connect+develop* website is found at secure3.verticali. net/pg-connection-portal/ctx/noauth/PortalHome.do.

26. October 2011, www.innocentive.com.

27. In the spring of 2011 the platform contained 12,000 ideas and more than 21,000 comments. Over 20,000 employees were at that point engaged in it. (Personal conversation with Magnus Karlsson, Director of New Business Development and Innovation at Ericsson.)

28. The quote is commonly attributed to Pablo Picasso, although TS Eliot among others is also alleged to have minted the same or a similar one.

29. Facts in this section are based on various sources, such as www.lowendmac.com and Walter Isaacson's excellent biography of Steve Jobs, *Steve Jobs*, Simon & Schuster, New York, 2011.

30. It's worth noting that history is full of successful companies built by people who didn't invent the original product. For instance, Lars Magnus Ericsson didn't invent the telephone. Still, less than 20 years after founding his company in 1876, Ericsson's products and services served markets in China, South Africa, Brazil and, of course, Sweden.

31. Ackoff, Russell Lincoln, *The Art of Problem Solving: Accompanied by Ackoff's Fables*, Wiley, New York, 1978. This material is reproduced with permission of John Wiley & Sons, Inc.

32. Although this quote is usually attributed to Aristotle, some academics claim it to be Will Durant's interpretation of Aristotle's *The Nichomachean Ethics*, expressed in Durant, Will, *The Story of Philosophy: The Lives and Opinions of the Greater Philosophers*, Garden City, New York, 1927.

33. The Chinese often attribute this quote to Xun Zi (312–230 BC), who was one of Confucius's followers.

34. This kind of presentation is called *cortical homunculus* and explains a lot of what we do with our hands and feet, how we learn through getting them (or our face) involved in what we do, and so forth. Google it or see en.wikipedia.org/wiki/Cortical_homunculus to learn more.

35. Johan Roos is Professor, MD and Dean at Jönköping International Business School and previously ran the research foundation *ImaginationLab* in Lausanne. The results from his research into Seriousplay were presented in September 2002 at the Strategic Management Society's annual conference in Paris.

36. See www.seriousplay.com for details.

37. Kurzweil, Ray, *The Age of Spiritual Machines: When Computers Exceed Human Intelligence*, Viking, New York, 1999.

38. Wilde, Oscar, *The Soul of Man Under Socialism and Selected Critical Prose*, Penguin Books, London, 2001.

39. For further information about Watson, see for instance www.nytimes.com/2010/06/20/magazine/20Computer-t.html.

40. This quotation is commonly attributed to Pablo Picasso, although its origin can't be confirmed.

41. Drucker, Peter Ferdinand, *Management Challenges for the 21st Century*, Butterworth-Heinemann, Oxford, 1999.

42. Goodell, Jeff, *The Cyberthief and the Samurai: The True Story of Kevin Mitnick-And the Man Who Hunted Him Down*, Dell Publishing, New York, 1996.

43. Both the size of Shimomura's engagement and the allegations against Mitnick has been debated and several books have been written on the topic.

44. Sun, Tzu, *The Art of War*, Oxford University Press, London, 1971.

45. For more data, see for instance the CIA factbook (www. cia.gov/library/publications/the-world-factbook/) or OECD.StatExtracts (stats.oecd.org).
46. For access to the data, download Kairos Future's *Global Values App* for iPhone at Apple's App-store.
47. For further details, visit www.pisa.oecd.org.
48. The First Opium War lasted between 1839 and 1842, and the second one between 1856 and 1860.
49. See for instance OECD's fact-blog on this topic (blog. oecdfactblog.org/?p=173) or visit the website in tribute to Angus Maddison's work (www.ggdc.net/maddison/ Maddison.htm).
50. Lian Si's book (*Yi zu: da xue bi ye sheng ju ju cun shi lu*) has so far only been published in Chinese.
51. Siwu, Chen and Yahong, Li, 'China's "ant tribe" between dreams and reality', *Asia Times*, Hong Kong, January 15, 2010, www.atimes.com/atimes/China/LA15Ad02. html.
52. For more information, see the BGC press release from September 2010 at www.bcg.com/media/ PressReleaseDetails.aspx?id=tcm:12-60402.
53. See Nataraj, Geethanjali, 'China spends 11% of GDP on infrastructure, India 6%', *The Financial Express*, March 4, 2010, www.financialexpress.com/news/china-spends-11-of-gdp-on-infrastructure-india-6/586401.
54. GBP 480 billion according to Moore, Malcolm, 'China steams ahead with world's fastest train', *The Telegraph*, February 13, 2010, www.telegraph.co.uk/ news/worldnews/asia/china/7230137/China-steams-ahead-with-worlds-fastest-train.html.
55. See Inhabitat blog; inhabitat.com/china-to-connect-its-high-speed-rail-all-the-way-to-europe. Used by permission from the blogger Bridgette Meinhold.

56. Moore, Malcolm, 'King's Cross to Beijing in two days on new high-speed rail network', *The Telegraph*, March 8, 2010, www.telegraph.co.uk/news/worldnews/asia/china/7397846/Kings-Cross-to-Beijing-in-two-days-on-new-high-speed-rail-network.html.

57. Original research based on openly available information from the two projects.

58. McGray, Douglas, 'Pop-Up Cities: China Builds a Bright Green Metropolis', *Wired Magazine*, April 24, 2007, www.wired.com/wired/archive/15.05/feat_popup.html.

59. For more information, see the BGC press release from September 2010 at www.bcg.com/media/PressRelease Details.aspx?id=tcm:12-60402.

60. See for instance Maddison, Angus, *Chinese economic performance in the long run*, 2. ed. rev. and updated, Development Centre of the Organisation for Economic Co-operation and Development, Paris, 2007. Here Maddison estimates China's share of GDP in 2030 to be 23 percent, and in 2003 to be 15.1 percent. Estimates by the World Bank, the IMF and the CIA are normally lower than Maddison's estimates.

61. Gunther, Marc, 'Warren Buffett takes charge', *CNNMoney*, April 13, 2009, money.cnn.com/2009/04/13/technology/gunther_electric.fortune.

62. In 2011 ZTE overtook Panasonic's position as number one in terms of applications for international patents. ZTE ended up as number three in the list and Ericsson ranked 10. See http://www.wipo.int/pressroom/en/articles/2012/article_0001.html.

63. See www.ericsson.com/ericsson/press/events/2010/business_innovation_forum/program_19.shtml.

64. C114, 'Ericsson says R&D key to winning China 3G orders', *C114*, May 27, 2009, www.cn-c114.net/577/a414946.html.

65. See for instance Thomas, L. G. & D'Aveni, Richard, *The Changing Nature of Competition in the US Manufacturing Sector, 1950 to 2002*, unpublished paper, 2009. This shows how within-industry heterogeneity in returns has risen quickly in the last 15 years due to increased competition.

66. Bradsher, Keith, 'China Drawing High-Tech Research from US', *The New York Times*, March 17, 2010, www.nytimes.com/2010/03/18/business/global/18research.html?hpw.

67. Ford, Henry, *My Life and Work*, William Heinemann, London, 1923.

68. Bloomberg Businessweek, 'The race to build really cheap cars', *Bloomberg Businessweek*, April 13, 2007, www.msnbc.msn.com/id/18097600/ns/business-us_business/t/race-build-really-cheap-cars/#.Tp80sXHGYXw.

69. Translation of Hugo, Victor, *Histoire d'un crime*, Calmann Lévy, Paris, 1877.

70. Brazil, Russia, India and China.

71. Being the new set of growth countries launched by HSBC CEO Michael Geoghegan in April 2010, CIVETS stands for Columbia, Indonesia, Vietnam, Egypt, Turkey and South Africa – all countries with high growth, growing populations and relatively stable political situations.

72. Fitzgerald, Michael, 'How Innovations from Developing Nations Trickle-Up to the West', *Fast Company*, March 1, 2009, www.fastcompany.com/magazine/133/as-the-world-turns.html.

73. Fast Company, 'Trickle-Up Trends', *Fast Company*, March 1, 2009, www.fastcompany.com/magazine/133/trickle-up-trends.html.

74. The sentence headed Bumrungrad International's website www.bumrungrad.com in January 2012.
75. See knowledge.wharton.upenn.edu/printer_friendly. cfm?articleid=2327 for an interview with the Bumrungrad director of marketing, Kenneth Mays.
76. Bradsher, Keith, 'China Drawing High-Tech Research from US', *The New York Times*, March 17, 2010, www.nytimes. com/2010/03/18/business/global/18research.html?hpw.
77. The topic of long-term cycles has been discussed by several researchers. The idea of 80-year cultural cycles was proposed in Strauss, William and Howe, Neil, *The Fourth Turning: An American Prophecy – What the Cycles of History Tell Us About America's Next Rendezvous with Destiny*, Broadway Books, New York, 1997. Economic historians such as Lennart Schön, Professor at Lund University, describe the economic waves as 40-year-long waves, while other economists tend to lean towards more traditional Kondratieff-cycles of 50–60 years. The concept of combined cultural, political and economic 80-year waves was developed by Jörgen Jedbratt and myself in the report *Allting går igen och ändå inte* (in Swedish), Kairos Future, 2002.

2   A NEW PARADIGM EMERGING

1. Of course, everyone in the world does not have Facebook or LinkedIn accounts. Facebook has fewer than 1 billion users, less than 1 in 6 of "everyone". LinkedIn is much less than this (<200 million users). But to that 300 million Sina Weibo accounts could be added, and in many groups, especially in the West, more or less "everyone" has different types of social meida accounts accounts.
2. Foster, Richard N. and Kaplan, Sarah, *Creative Destruction: Why Companies that are Built to Last Underperform*

the Market, and how to Successfully Transform them, 1. ed., Currency/Doubleday, New York, 2001.

3. Named by Ross Ashby himself in Ashby, W. Ross, *An Introduction to Cybernetics*, Chapman & Hall, London, 1956.

4. See the discussion on the topic in Miller, George, 'The Magical Number Seven, Plus or Minus Two: Some Limits on our Capacity for Processing Information', *Psychological Review*, vol. 63, no. 2, 1956.

5. Haeckel, Stephan H. and Nolan, Richard L., 'Managing by Wire', *Harvard Business Review*, vol. 71, no. 5, 1993.

6. For further information, see Lindgren, Mats and Bandhold, Hans, *Scenario Planning: The Link between Future and Strategy*, Rev. and updated ed., Palgrave Macmillan, Basingstoke, 2009.

3 THE THOUGHT ECONOMY

1. See his trilogy of the Information age, for instance Castells, Manuel, *The Rise of the Network Society*, 2. ed., Wiley-Blackwell, Chichester, West Sussex, 2010.

2. See for example Fuchs, Victor R., *The Service Economy*, National bureau of economic research, New York, 1968 or Gershuny, Jonathan, *After Industrial Society?: The Emerging Self-Service Economy*, Macmillan, London, 1978.

3. See for example Masuda, Yoneji, *The Information Society as Post-Industrial Society*, 2. pr., Washington, DC, 1983 or Hawken, Paul, *The Next Economy*, 1. ed., Holt, Rinehart and Winston, New York, 1983.

4. See for example Beck, Ulrich, *Risk Society: Towards a New Modernity*, Sage, London, 1992 or Giddens, Anthony, 'Risk and Responsibility', *Modern Law Review*, vol. 62, no. 1, 1999.

5. See for example Bell, Daniel, *The Coming of Post-Industrial Society: A Venture in Social Forecasting* [new edn], Penguin, Harmondsworth, 1976.

6. See for example Amin, Ash (ed.), *Post-Fordism: A Reader*, Blackwell, Oxford, 1994.

7. See for example Toffler, Alvin, *The Third Wave*, Collins, London, 1980.

8. See for example Jensen, Rolf, *The Dream Society: how the Coming Shift from Information to Imagination will Transform your Business*, McGraw-Hill, New York, 1999.

9. See for example Pine, B. Joseph and Gilmore, James H., *The Experience Economy: Work is Theatre & Every Business a Stage*, Harvard Business School, Boston, MA, 1999.

10. See for example Drucker, Peter Ferdinand, *The Age of Discontinuity: Guidelines to our Changing Society*, Harper & Row, New York, 1969.

11. Lindgren, Mats and Bandhold, Hans, *Scenario Planning: The Link between Future and Strategy*, Rev. and updated ed., Palgrave Macmillan, Basingstoke, 2009.

12. According to recent research, togetherness seems to be the new black. See for example Parks and Resorts' study on tomorrow's experiences, *Upplevelser i världsklass* (in Swedish), with research conducted by Kairos Future in 2011. For more information, visit www.parksandresorts.com/press.

13. Starbucks Coffee Company launched *My Starbuck Idea* in March 2008 and within one year they had received 70,000 ideas from customers. Visit mystarbucksidea.force.com for more information.

4 JAZZING UP THE DATA

1. Anderson, Chris, 'The End of Theory: The Data Deluge Makes the Scientific Method Obsolete', *Wired*, June 23,

2008, www.wired.com/science/discoveries/magazine/16-07/pb_theory#ixzz12HcgUVfA.

2. For instance, Swedish investment banks Erik Penser and Carnegie closed their trading departments in September 2011. See www.avanza.se/aza/press/press_article.jsp?article=209928 (in Swedish).

3. October 2011, www.facebook.com/press/info.php?statistics.

4. Facebook's projected revenue for 2011 is over four billion USD in 2011 – twice as much as in 2010 – most of it coming from advertising. See Womack, Brian, 'Facebook Revenue Will Reach $4.27 Billion, EMarketer Says', *Bloomberg*, September 20, 2011, www.bloomberg.com/news/2011-09-20/facebook-revenue-will-reach-4-27-billion-emarketer-says-1-.html.

5. Wray, Richard, 'Digital Sky Technologies takes $200m stake in Facebook', *The Guardian*, May 26, 2009, www.guardian.co.uk/business/2009/may/26/dst-facebook-zuckerberg-microsoft-milner.

6. The Financial Times has estimated the value of the expected Facebook IPO at more than USD 66.5 billion, based on recent individual shares sales. Dembosky, April, 'Facebook puts off IPO until late 2012', *Financial Times*, September 14, 2011, www.ft.com/intl/cms/s/2/2b842146-dec3-11e0-a228-00144feabdc0.html#axzz1YaZdbKnU.

7. Raice, Shaindy, 'Facebook Targets Huge IPO', *Wall Street Journal*, November 29, 2011, online.wsj.com/article/SB10001424052970203935604577066773790883672.html.

8. Oreskovic, Alexei, 'Exclusive: Facebook Doubles First-Half Revenue', *Reuters*, September 7, 2011, www.reuters.com/article/2011/09/08/us-facebook-idUSTRE7863YW20110908.

9. Salkowitz, Rob, 'Social Aggregators: Web 2.0's New Trick', *Internet Evolution*, June 3, 2009, www.internetevolution. com/document.asp?doc_id=177548&page_number=6.

10. Surowiecki, James, *The Wisdom of Crowds: Why the Many are Smarter than the Few*, Abacus, London, 2005.

11. Watch Surowiecki's TED-talk at www.ted.com/talks/ james_surowiecki_on_the_turning_point_for_social_ media.html.

12. Since 2009, the Swedish word *fredagsmys* (here translated to Cozy Friday) has been successfully framed by OLW – the Swedish snacks brand whose catchy jingle has made the word almost synonym with the brand. The usual fredagsmys in Swedish households doesn't only involve snacks, however, but also TV-watching and Mexican (!) or takeaway food. Watch the commercial that did it at www.olw.se or on YouTube (just search *fredagsmys*).

13. See for instance the reports by Kennedy Research & Consulting Advisory at www.kennedyinfo.com.

14. According to Bill Miller, Oracle's director of IT and MDM strategy and architecture, at a conference on analytics-driven strategy in San Francisco, January 2011.

15. For further information, see *China's Three Waves of Innovation – A Quantitative Study of China's New Invention Landscape*, Kairos Future, 2011.

16. See Naisbitt, John, Naisbitt, Nana and Philips, Douglas, *High Tech High Touch: Technology and our Search for Meaning*, 1. ed., Broadway, New York, 1999, or the earlier Naisbitt, John, *Megatrends: Ten New Directions Transforming our Lives*, Warner Books, New York, 1982 – the book in which he first talked about the concept. According to Wikipedia it has been published in 57 countries and sold more than 14 million copies.

17. See the report *Upplevelser i världsklass* (in Swedish), Parks and Resorts in cooperation with Kairos Future, 2011.
18. To learn more about Google Goggles, visit www.google. com/mobile/goggles.
19. Media agency Starcom presents the tool and the results of the promotion concept at www.starcom. se/content/case/2010-04-27/synsams-cheap-monday-%20clairvoyant.
20. The launch of Facebook's facial recognition spurred a tidal wave of negative integrity-related response. See for example www.pcworld.com/article/229742/why_ facebooks_facial_recognition_is_creepy.html.

5 WALTZING INTO THE FUTURE

1. Quote from The Left Hand of Darkness by Ursula K. Le Guin Copyright (c) 1969; used by permission of the author and the author's agents, the Virginia Kidd Agency, Inc.
2. Teece, David J. et al., 'Dynamic Capabilities and Strategic Management', *Strategic Management Journal*, vol. 18, no. 7, 1997.
3. Hamel, Gary and Valinkangas Liisa, 'The Quest for Resilience', *Harvard Business Review*, September 1, 2003.
4. Kim, W. Chan and Mauborgne, Renée, *Blue Ocean Strategy: How to Create Uncontested Market Space and Make the Competition Irrelevant*, Harvard Business School Press, Boston, MA, 2005.
5. Lovallo, Dan P. and Mendonca, Lenny T., 'Strategy's strategist: An interview with Richard Rumelt', *McKinsey Quarterly*, November 2007, www.mckinseyquarterly. com/Strategys_strategist_An_interview_with_Richard_ Rumelt_2039.

6. Exploring 25 factors related to management, strategy, process, culture and structure, the aim of my research then was to find the most important organizational attributes to overall performance in turbulent environments. See Lindgren, Mats, *Strategic Flexibility – Antecedents and Performance Implications*, Henley Management College/ Brunel University, Uxbridge, 2001.

7. In the 2000s Kairos Future has performed several studies on this topic, among others one involving marketing directors in major corporations and government bodies: *Pardigmskifte i omvärldsanalysen* (in Swedish), Kairos Future, 2004. In organizations where top managers actively promoted the activities 70 percent had a systematic and proactive approach to business environment analysis compared to 10 percent in organizations where such support was lacking.

8. For further information about Shell's widely admired CSR projects and policies, see www.shell.com/home/ content/environment_society.

9. Carroll, Lewis, *Alice's Adventures in Wonderland; and, Through the Looking-Glass and what Alice Found There*, Macmillan and Co., London, 1911.

10. Lakein, Alan, *How to Get Control of your Time and your Life*, P. H. Wyden, New York, 1973.

11. Clinton, Bill, *My Life*, Hutchinson, London, 2004.

12. According to people who knew her back then.

13. Fiegenbaum, Avi et al., 'Strategic Reference Point Theory', *Strategic Management Journal*, vol. 17, no. 3, 1996.

6 GETTING INTO THE SWING OF THINGS

1. The quotation is commonly attributed to Edison, although the context in that case remains unconfirmed.

According to the Edison Biotechnology Institute at the University of Ohio, it refers to Edison's failed experiments with storage batteries (see www.ohio.edu/biotech/about/edison.html).

2. Stern, Ithai and Henderson, Andrew D., 'Within-business diversification in technology-intensive industries', *Strategic Management Journal*, vol. 25, no. 5, 2004.

3. Kirchgeorg, Volker et al., 'Pathways to Innovation Excellence', *Arthur D. Little*, www.adl.com/uploads/tx_extthoughtleadership/ADL_InnoEx_Report_2010.pdf.

4. This model derives from my dissertation (Lindgren, Mats, *Strategic Flexibility – Antecedents and Performance Implications*, Henley Management College/Brunel University, Uxbridge, 2001) but has been further developed through thorough international business research presented in this and other chapters in the book.

5. For comparison of national cultures, see for instance www.geert-hofstede.com.

6. This is also what we have found in our international motivational research, for instance in the nine-country study previously mentioned.

7   IT TAKES TWO TO TANGO

1. Thompson, Christine, 'Apple Strategy & Corporate Culture — Proven Success Formula', *Musings: Content, Strategy, Marketing & Business*, June 20, 2010, www.informing-arts.biz/blog/apple-envy-what-does-it-take-to-be-like-apple.

2. You can download all *Manpower Work Life* studies (in Swedish) from www.manpower.se/mpnet3/Content.asp?NodeRef=51901&Ref=SWEDEN_NORDIC&LangID=se.

3. Download our *Global Values* iPhone app from Apple's App Store. For more information, see www.kairosfuture. com/globalvalues.

4. See *Generation Ambition* (in Swedish), Kairos Future, 2006.

5. McKinsey consultants Scott Keller and Colin Price recently built an organizational change model and dedicated a book to the theme. See Keller, Scott and Price, Colin, *Beyond performance*, John Wiley and sons, Hoboken, New Jersey, 2011.

6. This is of course an exaggeration, but compared to their older workmates young people normally have more of a mercenary approach to work, at least in the West.

7. This was one of the points already in Pine, B. Joseph and Gilmore, James H., *The Experience Economy: Work is Theatre & Every Business a Stage*, Harvard Business School, Boston, MA., 1999, where they called me-making 'transformation'. See also for instance Lindgren, Mats, Lüthi, Bernhard and Fürth, Thomas, *The me we Generation: What Business and Politics must Know about the Next Generation*, Bookhouse Publishing, Stockholm, 2005, where the young generation's balance between individualism and community is discussed in the context of a study of youth in the Nordic region.

8. These are results found in several studies that we have conducted over the years, among them the previously mentioned nine-country study and the recent research project *Managing Youth*, Kairos Future, 2011.

9. Figure 7.3 is an adapted version of a concept from Lindgren, Mats, Lüthi, Bernhard and Fürth, Thomas, *The me we Generation: What Business and Politics must*

Know about the Next Generation, Bookhouse Publishing, Stockholm, 2005.

10. Tree photo by *solaro* (via Flickr).
11. See *Managing Youth*, Kairos Future, 2011.
12. Boot camps has increasingly become a metaphor for tough feeback-based training, although it originally referred to US military recruit training.
13. See *Morgondagens Ledare* (in Swedish), Kairos Future, 2005.
14. See *Global Youth*, Kairos Future, 2009.
15. See *Successful Leaders*, Kairos Future, 2007.

8 DANCING CHEEK-TO-CHEEK

1. See *Upplevelser i världsklass* (in Swedish), Parks and Resorts, 2011, a report by Kairos Future. This is also in line with a recent update of Maslow's classical hierarchy of needs: Kenrick, Douglas T., et al., 'Renovating the Pyramid of Needs: Contemporary Extensions Built upon Ancient Foundations', *Perspectives on Psychological Science*, vol. 5, no. 3, 2010, www.csom.umn.edu/assets/144040.pdf.
2. Figure 8.1 is an adaptation of Pine and Gilmore's well-known model from Pine, B. Joseph and Gilmore, James H., *The Experience Economy: Work is Theatre & Every Business a Stage*, Harvard Business School, Boston, MA, 1999. The adaptation is published in *Upplevelser i världsklass* (in Swedish), Parks and Resorts, 2011.
3. See *Tomorrow's Sales*, Kairos Future, 2005.
4. This is one of the conclusions of our ongoing study of B2B-sales involving 600–700 Swedish top managers from major corporations in 2006 and 350 respondents in 2009. See *Successful Sales of the Future*, Kairos Future, 2006 and 2009.

9 BUILDING THE JAMMING ORGANIZATION

1. This is similar to (but not the same as) what Miles and Snow called a *prospector posture* in their seminal work in 1978. See Miles, Raymond E. and Snow, Charles C., *Organizational Strategy, Structure, and Process*, McGraw-Hill, New York, 1978.
2. For further information about the TRIM-process and Kraft Foods' application of it, see for instance Lindgren, Mats and Bandhold, Hans, *Scenario Planning: The link between Future and Strategy*, Rev. and updated ed., Palgrave Macmillan, Basingstoke, 2009.
3. Boulding, Kenneth E., *The Image: Knowledge in Life and Society*, Univ. of Michigan Press, Ann Arbor, 1956.
4. Polak's book *The Image of the Future* was written in Dutch in the early 1950s and translated by Elise Boulding. Polak, Frederik L., *The Image of the Future: Enlightening the Past, Orientating the Present, Forecasting the Future. Vol. 2, Iconoclasm of the Images of the Future, Demolition of Culture*, Sythoff, Leyden, 1961.
5. Bertil Strandberg, personal conversation.

BIBLIOGRAPHY

Ackoff, Russell Lincoln, *The Art of Problem Solving: Accompanied by Ackoff's Fables*, New York: Wiley, 1978.

Amin, Ash (ed.), *Post-Fordism: A Reader*, Oxford: Blackwell, 1994.

Anderson, Chris, 'The End of Theory: The Data Deluge Makes the Scientific Method Obsolete', *Wired*, June 23, 2008, www.wired.com/science/discoveries/magazine/16-07/pb_theory#ixzz12HcgUVfA.

Ashby, W. Ross, *An Introduction to Cybernetics*, London: Chapman & Hall, 1956.

Beck, Ulrich, *Risk Society: Towards a New Modernity*, London: Sage, 1992.

Bell, Daniel, *The Coming of Post-Industrial Society: A Venture in Social Forecasting* [new edn], Harmondsworth: Penguin, 1976.

Bloomberg Businessweek, 'The Race to Build Really Cheap Cars', *Bloomberg Businessweek*, April 13, 2007, www.msnbc.msn.com/id/18097600/ns/business-us_business/t/race-build-really-cheap-cars/#.Tp80sXHGYXw.

Boulding, Kenneth E., *The Image: Knowledge in Life and Society*, Ann Arbor: University of Michigan Press, 1956.

Bradsher, Keith, 'China Drawing High-Tech Research From US', *The New York Times*, March 17, 2010, www.nytimes.com/2010/03/18/business/global/18research.html?hpw.

Breathnach, Sarah B., *Simple Abundance: A Daybook of Comfort and Joy*, New York: Warner Books Inc, 1995.

Carroll, Lewis, *Alice's Adventures in Wonderland; and, Through the Looking-Glass and what Alice Found there*, London: Macmillan and Co., 1911.

Castells, Manuel, *The Rise of the Network Society*, 2 edn, Chichester, West Sussex: Wiley-Blackwell, 2010.

Clinton, Bill, *My Life*, London: Hutchinson, 2004.

Dembosky, April, 'Facebook puts off IPO until late 2012', *Financial Times*, September 14, 2011, www.ft.com/intl/cms/s/2/2b842146-dec3-11e0-a228-00144feabdc0.html#axzz1YaZdbKnU.

Dewey, John, *Democracy and Education: An Introduction to the Philosophy of Education*, New York: Macmillan, 1961.

Douglas T. Kenrick, Vladas, Griskevicius, Steven L. Neuberg and Mark, Schaller, 'Renovating the Pyramid of Needs: Contemporary Extensions Built upon Ancient Foundations', *Perspectives on Psychological Science*, vol. 5, no. 3, 2010, www.csom.umn.edu/assets/144040.pdf.

Drucker, Peter Ferdinand, *Management Challenges for the 21st Century*, Oxford: Butterworth-Heinemann, 1999.

Drucker, Peter Ferdinand, *The Age of Discontinuity: Guidelines to our Changing Society*, New York: Harper & Row, 1969.

Durant, Will, *The Story of Philosophy: The Lives and Opinions of the Greater Philosophers*, New York: Garden City, 1927.

Edgeworth, Francis Y., *Mathematical Psychics: An Essay on the Application of Mathematics to the Moral Sciences*, London: London School of Economics and Political Science, 1932 [1881].

Eisenberg, Bryan, 'Hidden Secrets of the Amazon Shopping Cart', *FutureNow*, February 26, 2008, www.grokdotcom.com/2008/02/26/amazon-shopping-cart.

Fast Company, 'Trickle-Up Trends', *Fast Company*, March 1, 2009, www.fastcompany.com/magazine/133/trickle-up-trends.html.

Ferrari, Giulio, Ferrari, Mario and Hempel, Ralph, *Building Robots with Lego Mindstorms: The Ultimate Tool for Mindstorms Maniacs!*, Rockland, MA: Syngress, 2002.

Feigenbaum, Avi, S. Hart and D. Schendel (1996). 'Strategic reference point theory.' *Strategic Management Journal* 17: 219–35.

Fitzgerald, Michael, 'How Innovations from Developing Nations Trickle-Up to the West', *Fast Company*, March 1, 2009, www.fastcompany.com/magazine/133/as-the-world-turns.html.

Ford, Henry, *My Life and Work*, London: William Heinemann, 1923.

Foster, Richard N. and Kaplan, Sarah, *Creative Destruction: Why Companies that are Built to Last Underperform the Market, and how to Successfully Transform them*, 1st edn, New York: Currency/Doubleday, 2001.

Fuchs, Victor R., *The Service Economy*, New York: National Bureau of Economic Research, 1968.

Gershuny, Jonathan, *After Industrial Society?: The Emerging Self-Service Economy*, London: Macmillan, 1978.

Giddens, Anthony, 'Risk and Responsibility', *Modern Law Review*, vol. 62, no. 1, 1999.

Goodell, Jeff, *The Cyberthief and the Samurai: The True Story of Kevin Mitnick-And the Man Who Hunted Him Down*, New York: Dell Publishing, 1996.

Gunther, Marc, 'Warren Buffett Takes Charge', *CNNMoney*, April 13, 2009, money.cnn.com/2009/04/13/technology/gunther_electric.fortune.

Haeckel, Stephan H. and Nolan, Richard L., 'Managing by Wire', *Harvard Business Review*, vol. 71, no. 5, 1993.

Hamel, Gary and Valinkangas Liisa, 'The Quest for Resilience', *Harvard Business Review*, September 1, 2003.

Hawken, Paul, *The Next Economy*, 1st edn, New York: Holt, Rinehart and Winston, 1983.

Hugo, Victor, *Histoire d'un crime*, Paris: Calmann Lévy, 1877.

Isaacson, Walter, *Steve Jobs*, New York: Simon & Schuster, 2011.

Jedbratt, Jörgen and Lindgren, Mats, *Allting går igen och ändå inte* (in Swedish), Stockholm: Kairos Future, 2002.

Jensen, Rolf, *The Dream Society: How the Coming Shift from Information to Imagination will Transform your Business*, New York: McGraw-Hill, 1999.

Kairos Future, *China's Three Waves of Innovation – A Quantitative Study of China's New Invention Landscape*, Stockholm, 2011.

Kairos Future, *Generation Ambition* (in Swedish), Stockholm, 2006.

Kairos Future, *Global Youth*, Stockholm, 2009.

Kairos Future, *Managing Youth*, Stockholm, 2011.

Kairos Future, *Morgondagens Ledare* (in Swedish), Stockholm, 2005.

Kairos Future, *Pardigmskifte i omvärldsanalysen* (in Swedish), Stockholm, 2004.

Kairos Future, *Successful Leaders*, Stockholm, 2007.

Kairos Future, *Successful Sales of the Future*, Stockholm, 2009.

Kairos Future, *Tomorrow's Sales*, Stockholm, 2005.

Parks & Resort, *Upplevelser i världsklass*, Stockholm, 2011 (report for Parks & Resorts).

Keller, Scott and Price, Colin, *Beyond Performance*, Hoboken, NJ: John Wiley, 2011.

Kim, W. Chan and Mauborgne, Renée, *Blue Ocean Strategy: How to Create Uncontested Market Space and make the Competition Irrelevant*, Boston, MA: Harvard Business School Press, 2005.

Kirchgeorg, Volker Markus Achtert and Hanno Großeschmidt, 'Pathways to Innovation Excellence', *Arthur D. Little*, www.adl.com/uploads/tx_extthoughtleadership/ADL_InnoEx_Report_2010.pdf.

Kiron, David and Shockley, Rebecca, 'The New Intelligent Enterprise: Creating Business Value with Analytics', *MIT Sloan Management Review*, Cambridge, MA: Sloan Management Review Association, 2011.

Kurzweil, Ray, *The Age of Spiritual Machines: When Computers Exceed Human Intelligence*, New York: Viking, 1999.

Lakein, Alan, *How to Get Control of your Time and your Life*, New York: P. H. Wyden, 1973.

Lindgren, Mats and Bandhold, Hans, *Scenario Planning: The Link between Future and Strategy*, Rev. and updated edn, Basingstoke: Palgrave Macmillan, 2009.

Lindgren, Mats, Lüthi, Bernhard and Fürth, Thomas, *The me we Generation: What Business and Politics must Know about the Next Generation*, Stockholm: Bookhouse Publishing, 2005.

Lindgren, Mats, *Strategic Flexibility – Antecedents and Performance Implications*, Uxbridge: Henley Management College/Brunel University, 2001.

Lorde, Audre and Hall, Joan W., *Conversations with Audre Lorde*, Jackson: University Press of Mississippi, 2004.

Lovallo, Dan P. and Mendonca, Lenny T., 'Strategy's Strategist: An Interview with Richard Rumelt', *McKinsey Quarterly*, November 2007.

Maddison, Angus, *Chinese Economic Performance in the Long Run*, 2nd edn, rev. and updated 960–2030 AD, Paris: Development Centre of the Organisation for Economic Co-Operation Development, 2007.

Masuda, Yoneji, *The Information Society as Post-Industrial Society*, 2. pr., Washington, DC: World future society, 1983.

McGray, Douglas, 'Pop-Up Cities: China Builds a Bright Green Metropolis', *Wired Magazine*, April 24, 2007, www.wired.com/wired/archive/15.05/feat_popup.html.

Miles, Raymond E. and Snow, Charles C., *Organizational Strategy, Structure, and Process*, New York: McGraw-Hill, 1978.

Miller, George, 'The Magical Number Seven, Plus or Minus Two: Some Limits on our Capacity for Processing Information', *Psychological Review*, vol. 63, no. 2, 1956.

Modis, Forecasting the Growth of Complexity and Change, Technological Forecasting & Social Change, 69, No 4, 2002.

Moore, Malcolm, 'China Steams Ahead with World's Fastest Train', *The Telegraph*, February 13, 2010, www.telegraph.co.uk/news/worldnews/asia/china/7230137/China-steams-ahead-with-worlds-fastest-train.html.

Moore, Malcolm, 'King's Cross to Beijing in Two Days on New High-Speed Rail Network', *The Telegraph*, March 8, 2010, www.telegraph.co.uk/news/worldnews/asia/china/7397846/Kings-Cross-to-Beijing-in-two-days-on-new-high-speed-rail-network.html.

Naisbitt, John, *Megatrends: Ten New Directions Transforming our Lives*, New York: Warner Books, 1982.

Naisbitt, John, Naisbitt, Nana and Philips, Douglas, *High Tech High Touch: Technology and our Search for Meaning*, 1st edn, New York: Broadway, 1999.

Nataraj, Geethanjali, 'China spends 11% of GDP on infrastructure, India 6%', *The Financial Express*, March 4, 2010, www.financialexpress.com/news/china-spends-11-of-gdp-on-infrastructure-india-6/586401.

Oreskovic, Alexei, 'Exclusive: Facebook Doubles First-Half Revenue', *Reuters*, September 7, 2011, www.reuters.com/article/2011/09/08/us-facebook-idUSTRE786 3YW20110908.

Pine, B. Joseph and Gilmore, James H., *The Experience Economy: Work is Theatre & Every Business a Stage*, Boston, MA: Harvard Business School, 1999.

Polak, Frederik L., *The Image of the Future: Enlightening the Past, Orientating the Present, Forecasting the Future. Vol. 2, Iconoclasm of the Images of the Future, Demolition of Culture*, Leyden: Sythoff, 1961.

Raice, Shaindy, 'Facebook Targets Huge IPO', *Wall Street Journal*, November 29, 2011, online.wsj.com/article/SB10001424052970203935604577066773790883672.html.

Salkowitz, Rob, 'Social Aggregators: Web 2.0's New Trick', *Internet Evolution*, June 3, 2009, www.internetevolution.com/document.asp?doc_id=177548&page_number=6.

Siwu, Chen and Yahong, Li, 'China's "ant tribe" between Dreams and Reality', *Asia Times*, Hong Kong, January 15, 2010, www.atimes.com/atimes/China/LA15Ad02.html.

Stern, Ithai and Henderson, Andrew D., 'Within-Business Diversification in Technology-Intensive Industries', *Strategic Management Journal*, vol. 25, no. 5, 2004.

Strauss, William and Howe, Neil, *The Fourth Turning: An American Prophecy – What the Cycles of History Tell Us About America's Next Rendezvous with Destiny*, New York: Broadway Books, 1997.

Sun, Zi, *The art of war*, London: Oxford University Press, 1971.

Surowiecki, James, *The Wisdom of Crowds: Why the Many are Smarter than the Few*, London: Abacus, 2005.

Teece, David J. Gary Pisano and Amy Shuen, 'Dynamic Capabilities and Strategic Management', *Strategic Management Journal*, vol. 18, no. 7, 1997.

Thomas, L. G. and D'Aveni, Richard, *The Changing Nature of Competition in the US Manufacturing Sector, 1950 to 2002* from 2009.

Thompson, Christine, 'Apple Strategy & Corporate Culture – Proven Success Formula', *Musings: Content, Strategy, Marketing & Business*, June 20, 2010, www.informing-arts.biz/blog/apple-envy-what-does-it-take-to-be-like-apple.

Toffler, Alvin, *The Third Wave*, London: Collins, 1980.

Wilde, Oscar, *The Soul of Man under Socialism and Selected Critical Prose*, London: Penguin Books, 2001.

Womack, Brian, 'Facebook Revenue Will Reach $4.27 Billion, EMarketer Says', *Bloomberg*, September 20, 2011, www.bloomberg.com/news/2011-09-20/facebook-revenue-will-reach-4-27-billion-emarketer-says-1-.html.

Wray, Richard, 'Digital Sky Technologies takes $200m Stake in Facebook', *The Guardian*, May 26, 2009, www.guardian.co.uk/business/2009/may/26/dst-facebook-zuckerberg-microsoft-milner.

INDEX

Page numbers followed by 'n' indicate notes.

A

Abele, Anton, 14–15, 59
Ackoff, Russell L., 25,
    171n31
adaptivity, 90, 97–9, 104
Adbusters, 18, 170n20
Adbusters magazine, 18,
    170n20
*The Age of the Spiritual
    Machines: When
    Computers Exceed
    Human Intelligence,*
    28–9, 172n37
alternative thinking, 96–7,
    103
Amazon, 2–3, 5, 169n1
ambitious team, talent
    excellence and, 127–8
Amim post-Fordism society,
    61, 178n6
analytics, 82
Anderson, Chris, 73,
    178n1

Ant Tribes, 33–4, 173n51
Apple, 24–5, 64, 116, 154,
    171n29, 171n30,
    183n1
Applied Materials, 46, 59
appreciation,
    importantance of,
    126
Aristotle, 26, 171n32
Armstrong, Lance, 6
Arthur D. Little, 105, 106,
    112, 183n3
Arup, 37, 174n58
Ashby's law of requisite
    variety, 55, 177n3
attitudes, of young people,
    123–4
automotive industry, car
    costing, 40–2

B

Bacon, Francis, 24
Bandhold, Hans, 155

B2B-companies, 139, 141
  partner-seeking trend in,
  140
B2C-companies, 139, 141
Beck risk society, 60,
  177n4
Bell post-industrial society,
  60, 178n5
Bergstrand, Nanne, 27, 59
Bezos, Jeff, 2
Bingham, Alpheus, 23
blog posts, 82
blogs, 8
Bloomberg Businessweek, 41,
  175n68
Boston Consulting Group
  (BCG), 34, 173n52,
  174n59
Boulding, Kenneth, 163,
  164, 186n3
brain-body coordination,
  28, 172n34
BRIC countries, 43, 175n70
Buffet, Warren, 39,
  174n61
Build Your Dreams (BYD),
  38–9, 174n61
Bumrungrad International
  Hospital, 45–6, 59,
  176n74, 176n75
Business 2.0, 13
business sense, sales
  excellence and, 147–9

Buy Nothing Day, 18,
  170n20
BYD. *see* Build Your Dreams
  (BYD)

C
Campogiani, Riccardo, 14
Carrol, Dave, 16–17, 59
Carroll, Lewis, 98, 182n9
Castells network society,
  60, 177n1
change, business and
  society, 1–47
  Adbusters magazine,
  17–18
  Ant Tribes (China), 33–4
  art of scoring, 26–7
  in automotive industry,
  40–2
  Bumrungrad
  International Hospital,
  45–6
  BYD (China), 38–9
  call for thinking, 30–1
  clinical information
  sites (PatientsLikeMe),
  12–13
  Dongtan project (China),
  37–8
  e-commerce market
  (Amazon) and, 2–3
  feelings (We Feel Fine),
  sites for, 10–11

Floatingsheep and, 7–8
Fujitsu, 19–20
giant leap for mankind, 25–6
in graphics (Gapminder), 5–6
high-speed rail project (China), 35–6
IBM, 29–30
infrastructure-development need, 34–5
InnoCentive, 22–4
innovation and (*see* innovation)
Internet and, 16–17
Kiva, 15–16
LEGO Mindstorms, 20–1
Mappiness website, 11–12
market research, value of, 39–40
match making and dating (OkCupid) sites and, 4–5
modern gardening and, 8–9
Pivot (Flake) and, 6–7
power of politics, 46–7, 176n77
Procter & Gamble, 21–2
recombination, 26
Stop Street Violence group, 14–15
in T-economy, 68, 69
treating employees, new way of, 42–3
trickles down, innovation, 43–5
United Airlines, 16–17
change excellence, 92–102. *see also* future-making; success factors
adaptivity and, 97–9, 104
alternative thinking and, 96–7, 103
competitive scanning and, 94–5, 103
cultural design and, 95, 103
opportunity scanning and, 95–6, 103
overview, 92–4
strategic conversation and, 99–100, 104
time horizons, importance of, 98–9
visionary proactivity and, 100–2, 104
China, 52
Ant Tribes in, 33–4
auto research centers, 40, 175n66
BYD in, 38–9
Dongtan project in, 37–8
in geopolitics, 38

China (*contd.*)
  greenhouse-emission in,
    38
  high-speed rail project of,
    35–6, 174n56
  infrastructure
    investments in, 34–5,
    173n53, 173n54
  market research for,
    Ericsson, 40
  Pisa-reports and, 32–3
  producer of scientific
    papers, 32
  share of global GDP, 38,
    174n60
  solar panels and, 46–7
  Tangjialing, 34
Citybanan project, 36,
  174n57
CIVETS countries, 43,
  175n71
clinical information, sites
  for, 12–13
Clinton, Bill, 99, 182n11
CNN Money, 13
co-creation, 108. *see also*
  innovation
collaboration
  performance and, 145–6
  sales excellence and,
    145–6
  talent excellence and,
    128–30

Collins, John Churton, 4
commitment, personal
  innovation and, 113–14
commodization, 139
competitive scanning,
  94–5, 103
complexity, 52–5
  effect of, 53
  external and internal,
    53–4
  levels of, 54, 55
  simplified, 54
Confucius, 28, 171n33
Connect+Develop (P&G), 22,
  106, 171n25
cortical homunculus,
  172n34
Coyne, Chris, 4
Cozy Friday, 81, 180n12
Creative, 24
creative climate,
  innovation and,
    112–13
culture
  design, 95, 103
  positive, talent excellence
    and, 130–1
  sales, 147
  transforming, 156–7
  work-life-balance
    preferences and,
    134–5
customer deficit, 139

customer insights,
    innovation and, 107–8
customer intimacy, 144,
    145. *see also* sales
    excellence
customer satisfaction,
    performance and, 76
customer understanding,
    sales excellence and,
    146
*The Cyberthief and the
    Samurai*, 31, 172n42

D
Daishonin, Nichiren, 5
Danone, 43–4
data, 73–89
    changes, computing
        power and, 7
    increasing amount of,
        73–4
    insight excellence
        (*see* insight excellence)
    measuring performance
        drivers, 75–8
    self-assessment, 87–9
    value of, 74–5
data-driven strategy, 95
data quality, insight
    excellence and, 79–81
dating sites (OkCupid), 4–5
d'Aveni, Richard, 40,
    175n65

da Vinci, Leonardo, 28
decision-making, 157
    implementation
        capability/speed, 110
    innovation and, 108–10
decisive leadership, 65, 66
development opportunities,
    talent excellence and,
    131–4
Digital Sky, 75, 179n5
Domino's Pizza, 17–18,
    172n19
Dongtan (China), 37
Doyle, Patrick, 18,
    172n19
Drucker knowledge
    economy, 61, 178n10
Drucker, Peter, 30–1,
    172n41
dynamic abilities, 90–1,
    181n2, 181n3, 181n4

E
e-commerce marketers
    (Amazon), 2–3
economic value, evolution
    of, 140–1, 185n2
Edgeworth, Francis Ysidro,
    11, 169n11
Edison, Thomas Alva, 105,
    110, 182n1
Eli Lilly, 13, 170n13
e-mail, 52

employee engagement. *see also* talent excellence
  drivers of, 125–6
  overview, 121
  from we-making to me-making activities, 122–3, 184n7
  work-life-balance issues and, 132–4
  young people and, 122–6, 184n6
employees satisfaction, 75–6
  importance of, 120–1
employer-employee relationship, 134–5
empowering leadership, 65, 66
engagement, employee. *see* employee engagement
Ericsson, 23, 39, 40, 171n27, 174n62, 174n63, 175n64
Ericsson, Lars Magnus, 171n30
Ethernet, 14
European Travel Commission, 86
The Experience Economy: Work is Theatre & Every Business a Stage, 184n7
external complexity, 53–4

F
Facebook, 8, 14, 45, 52, 74–5, 85, 179n3, 179n4, 179n5, 179n6, 179n7, 179n8, 181n20
Fadell, Tony, 24–5
FastCompany, 44, 175n72, 176n73
feedback, talent excellence and, 134–7
Fiegenbaum, Avi, 101, 182n13
Flake, Gary, 6–7, 169n6
Flannery, Matt, 15, 16, 59
Floatingsheep, 7–8, 59
focus shift, xix–xx
Ford, 41, 42, 85
Ford, Henry, 40–1, 42–3, 175n67
Fraunhofer Society, 24
Free Your Mind Award, 14
Fuchs service economy, 60, 177n2
Fujitsu, 19–20, 59
Fujitsu ScanSnap Scanner S300, 19–20
future capabilities, 153
  capital, 156–8, 159
future capability analysis, 154–5
future capability strategy, 154, 155

future capital, building, 152–5
capabilities, 153
future market capital, 158–62
internal capabilities, 156–8
market value and, 152
process, 154–5
products and offerings, 152
TRIM-process, 159–62, 186n2
Future Capital Index, 67
future capital model, 162–6
future capital navigator, 165–6
future dashboard, 166
future map, 165
future portfolio, 166
strategy map, 165
future dashboard, 166
future-making, 91
change excellence (*see* change excellence)
path to success, 91–2
self-assessment, 102–4
success factors, 93, 182n6
time horizons, importance of, 98–9
future map, 159–60, 161, 165

future market analysis, 154–5
future market capital, 158–62
future market strategy, 154, 155
future portfolio, 166
future products/offerings, 152
future strategist, xxi
future strategist leadership, 163–4
futurize, 67

G
game-changing deal, 21–2
Gapminder, 5, 7, 84
Gardena, 8
garden equipment producers, 8–9
gardening dimension jamming organization and, 57–8, 59
General Magic, 24
General Motors, 40, 85
general-to-specific approach, innovation and, 111
Generation Ambition, 120–1, 129, 184n4
generous gardeners, innovative companies as, 107

Geoghegan, Michael, 175n71
Gershuny service economy, 60, 177n2
Ghosn, Carlos, 41
Giddens risk society, 60, 177n4
Gilmore, James H., 184n7, 185n2
Global Values, 117, 183n3
Global Youth, 32, 133, 173n46, 185n13
Godell, Jeff, 31, 172n42
Google, 6, 8, 64, 85, 86–7, 128, 131, 181n18
Google+, 14
Google Goggles, 85, 181n18
Graham, Mark, 7
graphics, Rosling and, 5–6
greenhouse-emission, in China, 38
Gutierrez, Alejandro, 37, 174n58

H
hackers, Mindstorms and, 20–1
Hamel, Gary, 91, 181n3
Hammonds, Kristy Lynn, 17–18, 172n19
hard drive player, 24

Harmony Express (China), 36
Harris, Jonathan, 10–11, 169n10
Hawken information society, 60, 177n3
Haywood, John, 22
Henderson, Andrew D., 183n2
Heywood, Benjamin, 12, 59
Heywood, James, 12, 59
Heywood, Stephen, 12
High Tech High Touch, 84, 180n16
How to Get Control of Your Time and Your Life, 99, 182n10
Huawei, 39, 40
Hugo, Victor, 42, 175n69
Husqvarna, 8, 9, 59, 85–6
Husqvarna Global Garden Report 2010, 9, 169n8
Huston, Larry, 21, 22, 170n24
hypercompetition, 40

I
IBM, 29–30
ICT companies, 67, 107
The Image, 163, 186n3
implementation capability/ speed, innovation and, 108–10

India, infrastructure investments in, 35, 173n53

industrial economy, value-chain of, 62

infrastructure investments in China and India, 34–5, 173n53, 173n54

inhabitat weblog, 35, 173n55

innocent, being, 22–4

InnoCentive, 23, 171n26

innovation, 57. *see also* innovation excellence

dimensions, 156

at Ericsson, 23–4

general-to-specific approach, 111

InnoCentive, 23

large companies and, 23

overview, 105–6

at P&G, 21–2

rate, 53

revolutionary leaps in, 25–6

self-assessment, 114–15

in T-economy, 68, 69

trickles down, 43–5

innovation excellence

creative climate, 112–13

customer and user insights, 107–8

implementation capability, 108–10

overview, 107, 108

personal commitment, 113–14

supporting processes, 110–12

innovation machine, 111–12, 158–9

innovative companies

characteristics, 106–7

as generous gardeners, 107

as playful thinkers, 106

as serious players, 106–7

innovative leadership, 65, 66

insight, 68, 69

insight excellence, 78–87

data quality, 79–81

interpretational skill, 82–4

multi-competence, 84

open mind, 85–7

statistical methods, 82, 83

structured processes, 78–9

visualization, 84–5

Intel, 40

internal collaboration. *see also* collaboration

performance and, 145–6

sales excellence and, 145–6

internal complexity, 53, 54
Internet, 2, 16–17
Internet Evolution, 75
interpretational skill,
    insight excellence and,
    82–4
iPhone, 12, 106
iPod, 26, 106
iTunes, 25

J
Jackley, Jessica, 15, 16, 59
jamming organization,
    building, 55–9, 166–7
    future capability capital,
    156–8
    future capital model
    (from strategy to
    action), 162–6
    future market capital,
    158–62
    manager's role in, 56–7
    overview, 151
    21st century leadership
    (building future
    capital), 152–5
    strategic flexibility and
    performance, 57–8
    thinking, linking and
    blinking in T-economy,
    151–2
    thinking, playing and
    gardening for, 57–9

Jensen dream society, 61,
    178n8
Jeopardy!, 29, 30
Jin, David, 34
job(s), 116. *see also*
    employee engagement;
    talent excellence
    traits of, 117–20
Jobs, Steve, 24, 25, 59, 154
Jong, Erica, 20, 170n21
Joynt, Patrick, xv

K
Kairos Future, 8, 32, 56, 77,
    84, 86, 160, 181n17,
    181n7, xiv
Kalmar, 26–7
Kalmar FF, 27
Kamvar, Sam, 10–11, 169n10
Karlsson, Magnus, 171n27
Keller, Scott, 184n5
Kempe, Frans, 42
Kennedy Research &
    Consulting Advisory,
    180n13
Kierkegaard, Søren, 19
Kim, W. Chan, 91, 181n4
Kiva, 15–16, 170n15
knowledge worker
    productivity, 30–1
Kraft Foods, 160–1, 186n2
Krohn, Max, 4
Kurzweil, Raymond, 29

L

Lafley, A. G., 20–2, 59
Lakein, Allen, 99–100,
    182n10
Lasn, Kalle, 18
leadership
    future strategist, 163–4
    styles, 65–6
    thought, 65–6
LEGO Mindstorms, 20–1
LegOS, 20, 59, 65
LEGO Seriousplay, 28,
    172n36
Le Guin, Ursula K., 90,
    181n1
Lian Si, 33, 173n50
Liisa, Valinkangas, 91,
    181n3
LinkedIn, 14, 52
listening leadership, 65, 66
Live Labs (Microsoft), 6
London School of
    Economics, 11,
    170n12
Lorde, Audre, 10, 169n9

M

managers
    from emerging markets,
        66
    in jamming organization,
        56–7
    in mature markets, 65

Manpower Work Life, 116,
    117, 128–9, 130, 131,
    132, 183n2
Mappiness project, 11–12,
    85
Marabou Premium, 160–1
Marchant, Emmanuel, 44
market research, value of,
    39–40
Markoff, John, 31
Masuda information
    society, 60, 177n3
match making sites
    (OkCupid), 4–5
Mauborgne, Renée, 91,
    181n4
McDonalds, 18
McKinsey, 37, 44, 53,
    176n1, 184n5
Metcalfe, Robert, 14
Metro, 147
Microsoft, 6
Miller, Bill, 180n14
Miller's law, 55–6
Mindstorms, 20–1
Mindstorms NXT, 21
Mitnick, Kevin, 31,
    172n43
Mizner, Wilson, 169n2
Model T Ford, 41
Modis, Theodore, 168n1,
    xix, xviii
Mo & Domsjö, 42–3

Möller, Margareta
Finnstedt, 8
Moore's law, 98
Motion Chart Google
Gadget, 6
Motorola, 39
multi-competence, insight
excellence and, 84
Myers-Brigg test, 4
My Life, 99, 182n11
MySpace, 4–5

N
Naisbitt, John, 84, 180n16
Netscape, 2
New World
modern markets demand,
144
Old World to,
paradigmatic shifts,
48–52
performance drivers in,
77
Nokia, 39, 44–5
Nordic eyeglasses, 85
Novartis, 13, 170n13

O
OECD. *see* Organisation for
Economic Co-operation
and Development
(OECD)
OkCupid, 4–5, 85, 169n3

OkTrends, 4
Old World
to New World,
paradigmatic shifts,
48–52
time horizons,
importance of, 98–9
OODA Loop, pilots with,
56
open mind, insight
excellence and, 85–7
open source innovation,
108. *see also*
innovation
operational efficiency,
76–7
aspects of, 77
Opium Wars, 32, 173n48
opportunity scanning,
95–6, 103
performance and, 96, 97
Organisation for Economic
Co-operation and
Development (OECD),
32, 173n47, 173n49

P
paradigm, new, 48–59
building jamming
organization
(*see* jamming
organization, building)
choosing perspectives, 59

complexity
(*see* complexity)
Old World to New World
shift, 48–52
Parks and Resorts, 140
partner intimacy, 144. *see
also* sales excellence
partner management
internal collaboration
and, 145–6
sales excellence and,
143–5
PatientsLikeMe, 12–13, 85,
170n13
performance
clarity and, 135–6
collaboration and, 145–6
implementation speed
and, 109–10
organizational practices
and, 112–13
process focus and, 143
systematic opportunity
scanning and, 96, 97
performance drivers,
measuring, 75–8
personal commitment,
innovation and,
113–14
perspectives, selection of,
59
Petabyte Age, 73
Phillips, 24

Picasso, Pablo, 25, 30,
171n28, 172n40
PIGS countries, 47
Pine, B. Joseph, 184n7,
185n2
Pine & Gilmore experience
economy, 61, 178n9
Pinto, Mark R., 46, 47,
175n76
Pisa-reports, OECD, 32,
173n47
Pivot, 6–7, 84
playful thinkers,
innovative companies
as, 106
playing dimension,
jamming organization
and, 57, 58–9
Polak, Fred, 163, 164,
186n4
politics, power of, 46–7,
176n77
PortalPlayer, 24–5
positive culture, talent
excellence and, 130–1
PowerPoint, 5–6, 83
preferences, of young
people, 123–4
Price, Colin, 184n5
process focus
performance and, 143
sales excellence and,
142–3

Procter & Gamble (P&G),
21–2, 59, 64, 65, 106
production era, 139–40. *see
also* sales excellence
Proudfoot, Kekoa, 20,
170n22
Public Data Explorer, 6

R
Randén, Sofie, 160
raw material era, 139
recombination, 26
Renault-Nissan, 41, 42
Roos, Johan, 28, 172n35
Rosling, Hans, 5–6, 59,
169n5
Rudder, Christian, 4
Rumelt, Richard, 91, 181n5

S
sales
culture, 147
in T-economy, 68, 69
sales excellence, 141–9
business sense and,
147–9
customer understanding
and, 146
internal collaboration
and, 145–6
overview, 141–2
partner management
and, 143–5

process focus and, 142–3
sales culture and, 147
self-assessment, 149–50
Salkowitz, Rob, 75, 180n9
Samsung, 39
Scania, 25
*Scenario planning – the
link between future
and strategy,* 61, 155,
178n11
Schmalz, Bill, 18
self-assessment
future-making, 102–4
innovation and, 114–15
Petabyte age and, 87–9
sales excellence, 149–50
talent excellence, 137–8
in T-economy, 68–72
serious players, innovative
companies as, 106–7
service sectors, in USA, 32,
173n45
Setzer, Michael Anthony,
17–18, 172n19
seven number, in culture,
56, 177n4
Shanghai Expo 2010, 37
Shanghai Industrial
Investment
Corporation, 37
Shell, 96, 182n8
Shimomura, Tsutomu, 31,
172n43

simplified complexity, 54
social media, 14–15
  on business, 16–17
  revolution, 52
Sörenstam, Annika, 100–1,
  182n12
SoundJam MP, 25
South Korea, 52
Southwest Airlines, 16
SparkMatch, 4
speed
  implementation,
    innovation and, 110
  manager's ability, 56,
    177n5
Starbucks, 65, 178n13
Starcom, 181n19
statistical methods, insight
  excellence and, 82, 83
Stern, Ithai, 183n2
*Stop Street Violence (Stoppa
  gatuvåldet)*, 14
Strandberg, Bertil, 166,
  186n5
strategic conversation,
  99–100, 104
Strategic Reference Point
  Theory, 101, 182n13
strategy map, future capital
  navigator, 165
structured processes,
  insight excellence and,
  78–9

success factors, 93, 107,
  141, 182n6. *see also*
  change excellence;
  future-making
  adaptivity, 97–9, 104
  alternative thinking,
    96–7, 103
  competitive scanning,
    94–5, 103
  cultural design, 95, 103
  opportunity scanning,
    95–6, 103
  strategic conversation,
    99–100, 104
  visionary proactivity,
    100–2, 104
Sun Tzu, 32, 172n44
supporting processes,
  innovation and,
  110–12
Surowiecki, James, 75,
  180n10, 180n11
Synsam, 85, 181n19

T
TAIDA, 56, 168n1, xiv
talent excellence, 126–7.
  see also employee
  engagement
  ambitious team and,
  127–8
  collaboration and,
  128–30

talent excellence (*contd.*)
    development
        opportunities and,
        131–4
    feedback and, 134–7
    positive culture and,
        130–1
    self-assessment, 137–8
talent, in T-economy, 68,
    69
Tangjialing, 34
Tata, 39
Tata Motors, 41, 42
Tata Nano, 41
teamwork. *see also* talent
    excellence
    ambitious team, 127–8
    engagement and, 121–2
        (*see also* employee
        engagement)
    feedback and, 134–5
technological innovation,
    107–8
T-economy. *see* thought
    economy (T-economy)
TED conference, 5, 6
Teece, David J., 90, 181n2
Telegraph, 35–6, 174n56
thespark.com, 4
thinking dimension,
    jamming organization
    and, 57, 58
third wave, 82, 180n15

Thompson, Christine, 116,
    183n1
thought-cells, 61–5
thought economy
    (T-economy), 2, 60–72,
    102, 114, 149, 156,
    162, 164, 166
    performance drivers in, 77
    principles for successful
        management, 66–8
    self-assessment,
        68–72 (*see also* self-
        assessment)
    thinking, linking and
        blinking in, 151–2
    thought-cells and
        thought-nets, 61–5
    thought leadership for,
        65–6
    value-chain in, 62–3
thought leadership, 65–6
thought-nets, 61–5
thought productivity, 31
Through the Looking-Glass,
    98, 182n9
time horizons, importance
    of, 98, 99
Toffler third wave, 61,
    178n7
togetherness, 140
Toyota, 3, 25
transformation, 139
    B2B-sales, 140

Trendalyzer software, 6
Trend and Innovation
Management (TRIM)
process, 159–62,
186n2
trickles down, innovation,
43–5
TRIM process. *see* Trend
and Innovation
Management (TRIM)
process
Twain, Mark, 13, 170n14
21st century leadership,
152–5. *see also* future
capital, building
future capabilities, 153
future products and
offerings, 152
Twitter, 8, 45

U
United Airlines, 16–17
United breaks guitars, 16–17
user insights, innovation
and, 107–8

V
value-chain
of industrial economy,
62
in T-economy, 62–3
Village Enterprise Fund,
15

visionary leadership, 65, 66
visionary proactivity,
100–2, 104
visualization, insight
excellence and, 84–5
Volkswagen, 40

W
Wang Chuanfu, 59
Wang Mengshu, 36
Watson, 29–30, 172n39
Web-based supporting
systems, 162
We Feel Fine, 10–11, 85
Wikipedia, 6, 29, 52
Wilde, Oscar, 21, 29,
170n23, 172n38
Wired Magazine, 2, 19, 73,
178n1
The Wisdom of Crowds, 75,
180n10
'work-as-one' concept,
147
work-life-balance issues
employee engagement
and, 132–4
work satisfaction. *see also*
employees satisfaction;
job(s)
engagement and
(*see* employee
engagement)
importance of, 120–1

Y

Yagan, Sam, 4

young people
  attitudes and preferences
    of, 123–4
  engagement and,
    122–6, 184n6
    (*see also* employee
    engagement)

YouTube, 5, 16–17, 18,
  170n17, 170n18,
  172n19

Yunus, Mohammad, 15

Z

Zook, Matthew, 7

ZTE, 39, 174n62

Zuckerberg, Mark, 74